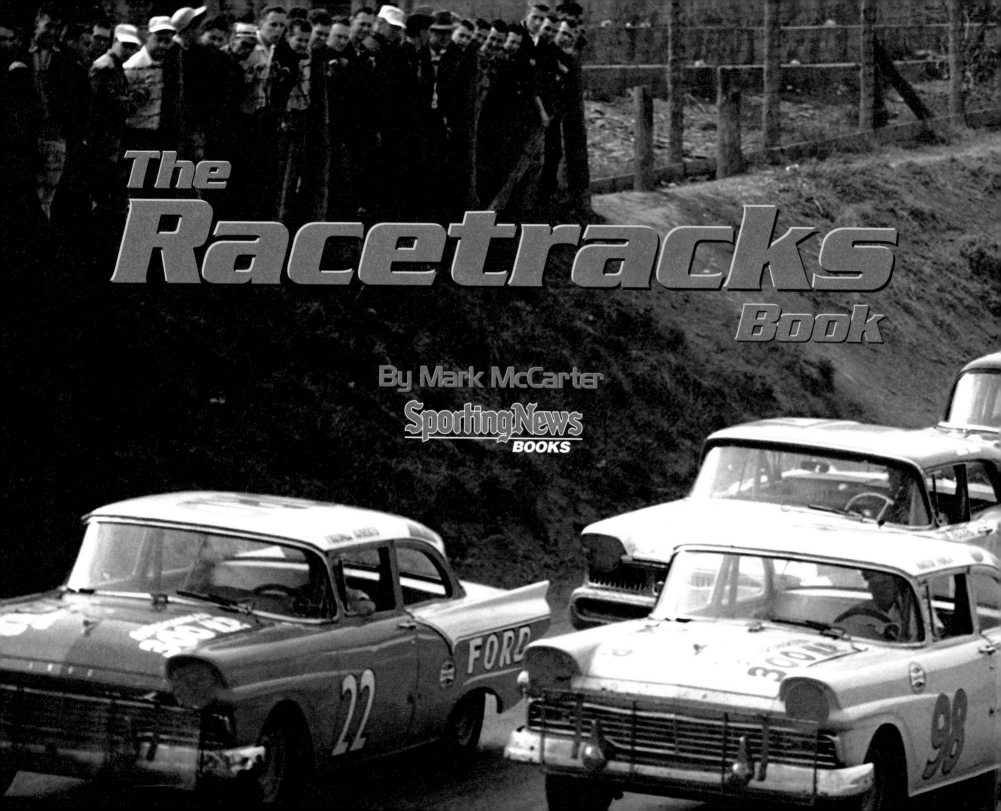

The Racetracks Book

By Mark McCarter

SportingNews
BOOKS

Photo Credits

T = Top   B = Bottom   L = Left   R = Right

Acknowledgements

Like a well-oiled pit crew, the process of producing this book came together quickly and efficiently, due to a dedicated group of people:

From conceptualization to actual work on the product, SPORTING NEWS editors Dale Bye, Paul Grant, Steve Meyerhoff and Jim Gilstrap made sure the words in this book were carefully edited and ready for publication. Photo editor August Miller collected and selected hundreds of images, and art director Michael Behrens put the words and pictures together with the help and guidance of creative director Bob Parajon.

The production staff led by Steve Romer and including Vern Kasal, Pamela Speh, Dave Brickey and Russ Carr put on the finishing touches, toning and polishing the entire package. And brought it all, we think, into the winner's circle.

I am also indebted to a lifetime of friends and associates inside of NASCAR and out—starting with Frank and Dot McCarter, who bought me my first typewriter to help start this odyssey, and Jordan McCarter, for whom I type. Patricia Cavanaugh Stumb provided editing and patience. The late Conner Gilbert was never far from mind. Among the many others to be thanked are Ken Patterson, Drew Brown, Jim Freeman, Joe Distelheim, Eli Gold, Ronnie White, John Pruett, Benny Parsons, Tom Roberts, Jon Edwards, Nealie Hamilton, the NASCAR quartet of Mike Helton, Jim Hunter, Danielle Frye and Herb Branham and the good ol' boys back at the shop, *The Huntsville Times* folks who tolerated the author's AWOL moments.

—MARK MCCARTER

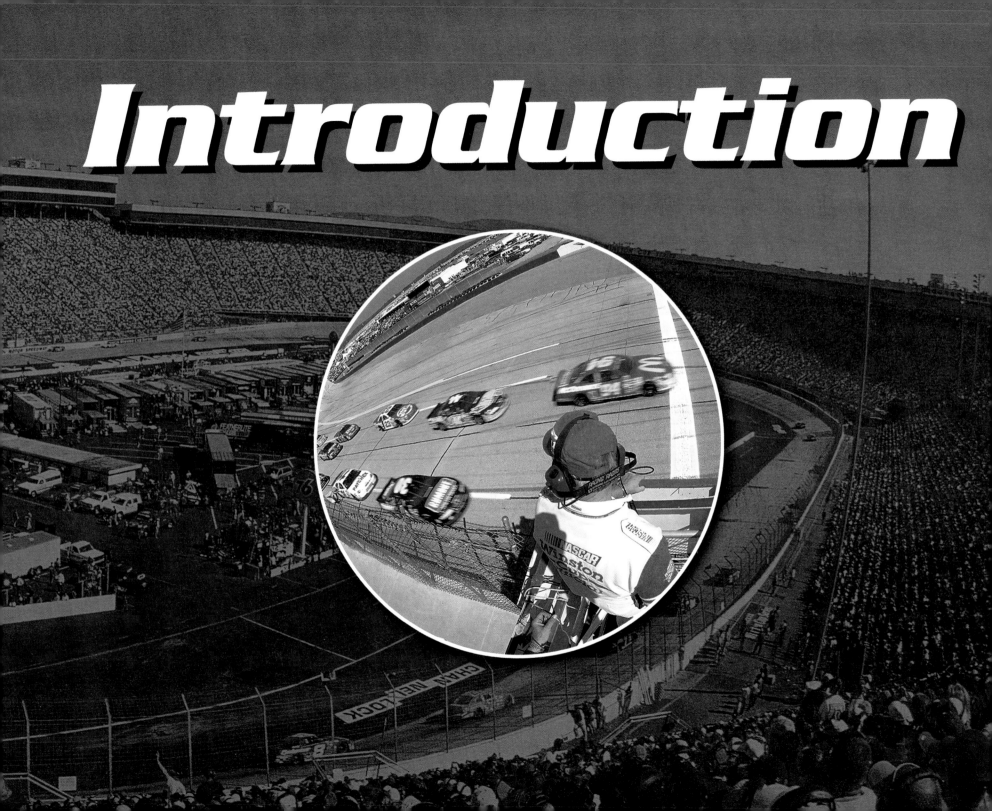

Introduction

Racetracks
Now, yesterday and forever

We figured if we turned the empty, enormous, red-and-white striped garbage barrel upside down, we could use it to boost ourselves up. My friend Doug and I could clamber from there to the roof of the concession stand. We could hoist up our cooler and our bucket of Kentucky Fried Chicken.

What a view! It will never get any better than this, we figured.

We sat there for probably an hour, at this enviably unique vantage point to watch the Atlanta 500. Nobody seemed to care. No officious track officials to order us down. No security guards. No problems. It was 1975 or so. There weren't enough people there to care.

It was called Atlanta International Raceway in those days, a little rough and frayed around the edges. Then again, so was the sport. I was just a fan, a young newspaper guy mostly covering stick-and-ball sports. Atlanta and Talladega were fun diversions close to home, mostly going with a carload of buddies to the infield for play time.

Talladega would, in future years in the newspaper world, become my unofficial "home track" as I began covering the sport on a regular basis. It is Atlanta, however, that I look at as somewhat symbolic—for myself, and, much more importantly, for NASCAR's growth in attention and amenities.

Twenty years after perching on the concession-stand roof, Doug and I were staying in the luxury condominium of a mutual friend, six stories high overlooking Turn 4. We could pull the

The cars may look different, and they certainly go faster now, but racing is racing, whether it was 1967 or 2003.

Over time, the racing surfaces have become more sophisticated and the protective walls have become more forgiving. Like the cars themselves, tracks have undergone an evolution, but nose-to-tail, door-to-door racing has been a constant, especially at the big tracks like Talladega.

blinds and park with our early-morning beverage in theater-style seats, gazing out the massive tinted window at the campers in the infield. The people we once were. The people we very much still were—except a little better-connected two decades later. We could munch on catered meals, sit in butter-soft black leather chairs in front of a giant-screen television to watch the race replays.

We even, one day, tried to figure where that old concession stand was before the massive renovation of the speedway.

We were hardly high-rollers. But some folks in the condo were. And NASCAR had become acutely aware how essential these folks would be to the sport's growth, stability and finances. These were the folks long spoiled by fancy skyboxes at football and baseball stadiums and basketball arenas. NASCAR began to construct more venues geared to them, more facilities at existing venues to cater to them. The evolution in phrasing, perhaps, from racetrack to speedways, just as basketball went from gyms to arenas, baseball from ballparks to stadiums (and, thankfully, these days, back to ballparks again).

Atlanta has many significant moments for me.

I watched solemnly, prayerfully, one afternoon there when a racer friend was loaded carefully into an ambulance, to be transported to a helicopter and then to a hospital. But the injuries suffered when his car plowed at an awkward angle into the outside wall were essentially instantly fatal.

I got behind the wheel of a stock car here, when Andy Hillenburg invited me to his FastTrack school. By day's end, I was turning laps at 140 mph or so. Of course, like the size and weight of a fish that got away grows exponentially each time an angler retells the story, honesty compels me to confess it was probably

On November 15, 1992, at Atlanta Motor Speedway, the racing career of the legendary Richard Petty came to a close, and the racing career of another legend—Jeff Gordon—began.

closer to 130 mph. I became acutely aware of how much I'd like to race cars—and how impossible it would be.

I was there November 15, 1992, when Richard Petty drove his final NASCAR Winston Cup race and the tightest points battle in history was settled. The asterisk attached to that day, and it grows ever larger all the time, was that Jeff Gordon made his Winston Cup debut, with little fanfare. Ten years after the fact, I asked Petty about that.

"We ended up a career, and he started a career," Petty said. "He took up the gap. I never really thought that much about it, but when you look back at it, it was the changing of a dynasty, more or less."

Much more quietly, another brief career started at that race, not even meriting a footnote. I began a hiatus from the newspa-

Though Indianapolis is a relatively new stop on the NASCAR circuit, the track has always been considered a classic by drivers.

per business that day. It was the first of some 60-plus races I would attend over the course of two seasons as a public-relations man, working alongside Michael Waltrip.

My eternal gratitude goes to Michael for two memorable years of fun and friendship. My bookshelf at home still holds a replica of his old yellow Pennzoil Pontiac. I cherish a cap he autographed for me at Bristol, his first win with me "on the team." It was the day he proposed to Buffy in victory lane.

• • •

The first great speedway is a mere 2,000 years old.

The Roman Circus Maximus, historians tell us, seated upward of 250,000 spectators. It was built into a hillside in Rome, and hairpin shaped, some 2,000 feet in length, 650-feet wide. Think Martinsville, but with U-turns at the end of each lap rather than a continuous oval. The structure was first timber, then reinforced with timber and stone. The racing surface was sand, all the better to soak up the blood.

Racers would run seven laps around the *spina*. Each lap was measured by movable emblems in the center of the oval, tilted slightly one after the other to help spectators keep track.

There was even a Richard Petty type: Gaius Apuleis started 4,257 races and won 1,462 of them over a 24-year period. The races appealed to the blood-and-guts type that also frequented the gladiator events in the Colosseum, but they were also a major social event. The fans dressed in their finest robes and garnished themselves with jewelry.

There was even the first skybox in history: The Emperor's palace was adjacent to the Circus Maximus, and he watched races from a special box in the palace.

Looks like the condos Bruton Smith built at Charlotte and Atlanta and Texas aren't such novel ideas after all.

As things moved from horses to horsepower centuries later, auto manufacturers looked for places to test their new inventions. They soon discovered people enjoyed watching those tests; they were even more popular when they pitted manufacturer against manufacturer. The auto industry then noticed a swelling in sales when cars were most successful on the track. Testing is what gave birth to the Indianapolis Motor Speedway in 1909. Hundreds of imitations were spun from there.

They may have been bold initiatives like Darlington, NASCAR's seminal speedway, or the clay and dirt ovals that stretched from every corner of the country, or the serpentine road courses for tiny sports cars. They may have been for good ol' boys who painted a shoe polish number on the side of the souped-up family sedan, or for ascot-wearing "sportsmen." But they all served a basic human need: for a man to prove he's a little faster and a little braver than the next man. Testosterone, as much as gasoline, fuels racecars.

At racetracks around the country, such as this victory at Daytona in 1964, Richard Petty was—is—The King. He helped fuel the sport to the level it has reached today.

And commerce fuels the sport. It became big business.

Look no further than NASCAR's most important speedway in terms of history and prestige. Daytona International Speedway was built because its predecessor made it difficult to charge fans.

Ormond Beach, just north of Daytona, became a hot spot in the early 1900s for drivers to set speed records on the hard-packed sand. It brought to Florida icons of racing history like Barney Oldfield and Ralph DePalma. When Bonneville Salt Flats in Utah proved to be a better proving ground, Daytona officials looked for another promotional tool. They encorporated the beach strip with Highway AIA for a long oval course. In March 1936, some 20,000 watched the first organized auto race on the beach.

Many of the tracks that held NASCAR races in the 1950s, such as Martinsville, remain active today.

However, promoters—including Bill France Sr.—would find themselves unable to assure each of the fans paid admission. Though fences were rigged around the track, it became easy for gate-crashers to sneak through sand dunes and pieces of scrub-covered property.

Then—an idea! A promoter placed a sign warning of rattlesnakes in that undeveloped property. The locals knew better, but visitors to the area heeded the warning and shelled out money for legitimate entrance.

By this time, France had created NASCAR, and its "Strictly Stock" division opened in 1949. It is the direct ancestor of Winston Cup racing as we now know it.

The circuit criss-crossed the country. It held races as far-flung as South Dakota and Oregon and Ontario, Canada in the 1950s. But clearly the strong roots of the sport were digging deeper into the Carolinas, and many places where NASCAR races were held in the 1950s—Charlotte, Richmond, Rockingham, Martinsville, Darlington—remain active today, though some cities

Racing at Darlington is always special, one of the reasons it's one of the classic tracks in use today.

have newer or different tracks.

The 1960s brought an almost absurd racing schedule—in 1964, there were 62 points races—before things were pared back late in the decade to a sport more closely resembling what it is today. Talladega Superspeedway, designed to be a faster cousin to Daytona, opened in 1969 in a maelstrom of controversy. It certainly wasn't unique for NASCAR to race out of the south, but Pocono, Michigan and Dover provided strong footholds in those regions. Other tracks came and went. Ontario, Calif. Texas World Speedway. Riverside, Calif. North Wilkesboro. Victims of progress, or poor management.

The late 1980s and early 1990s included expansion into Phoenix, New Hampshire and, in stunning circumstances, to Indianapolis Motor Speedway, heretofore the sacred ground where only the Indianapolis 500 was contested.

Las Vegas, like perhaps no other city in America can, has added its own unique flair to the circuit.

"We bring a different type of racing. We are the show! We go bumper-to-bumper and door handle-to-door handle," Darrell Waltrip said when the inaugural Brickyard 400 was announced in 1994. "They won't have to worry about mowing the grass when we're done and they may have to redo the walls." Ol' D.W. also said with sobering reverence, "The sacred halls of this place give me cold chills like I've never experienced before."

As the decade grew older, NASCAR's expansion brought few cold chills. There was little about which to be reverent.

A racing P.R. pal, Drew Brown, offered the teasing challenge when he learned of this book. "I dare you to write a book about NASCAR tracks and not use the phrase 'cookie-cutter.' "

Sorry. It can't be done.

The late 1990s brought the cookie-cutter tracks—1.5 mile trio-vals that seemed all alike. Texas. Chicagoland. Homestead-Miami. Kansas. Las Vegas. They all seemed cloned from Charlotte and Atlanta. Even California, at 2 miles, was a spin-off of Michigan.

Watch an old "classic" race rebroadcast on TV, and any devout fan can tell if it's Darlington or Daytona or Richmond, almost immediately. Watch one live on TV from Kansas, and you think it's Chicago. Or—wait. Were those palm trees behind the wall? Maybe it's Miami.

NASCAR had, whether intentionally or not, mimicked baseball of the 1960s, when so many round, multipurpose stadiums appeared on the landscape as if landing from another galaxy. Riverfront Stadium in Cincinnati. Three Rivers in Pittsburgh. Busch Stadium in St. Louis. Veterans Stadium in Philadelphia. Fulton-County Stadium in Atlanta. NASCAR should know that only one, Busch Stadium, will be in operation after 2003.

Unquestionably, it has been to NASCAR's benefit to branch out and tap larger, fresher, less-saturated marketplaces. It may be sad to say a farewell to North Wilkesboro and to fear for the future of Darlington, but, "I think it's for the best," says Benny Parsons, the former Winston Cup champ and now broadcaster. "We need to spread out."

That doesn't mean Parsons is a fan of the photocopied blue-prints apparently used everywhere.

"The races are better when it's a mechanical grip, not an engi-neered grip," Parsons says. Translation: Better races are won by set-up and human calculations, not by some sleek design that is perfected in a wind tunnel. "The better races are where the grip is changed by a combination of aero and mechanical. You go to

Atlanta was the mold for many of the cookie-cutter tracks that popped up in the 1990s.

Racing's growing popularity is evident at stops like Phoenix, where the stands are regularly filled.

those cookie cut- ... " Parsons stops and catches himself, "those mile-and-a-half tracks, and everything you do is aerodynamics."

But—like being flushed from the brush by rattlesnakes—fans hurry to those tracks in droves.

I'm a stadium freak.

You spend most of your adult life as a sportswriter, it helps. It's much more conducive to a happy life to have an appreciation, almost reverence, for stadiums, rather than simply an acceptance of them. There is enough sameness in our worlds—another stretch of freeway, another landscape painting above still another paisley bedspread in still another hotel room, another metal and plastic seat in an airport terminal—to make it advisable to savor the stadiums.

Maybe it's a high school football stadium in Bristol, Tenn., with the feel of a medieval castle. Or a rustic baseball diamond in a Dominican Republic barrio, with the locals wagering on every pitch. Or a stroll into Monument Park three hours before a World Series game at Yankee Stadium. Or sneaking a peek at Duke's basketball practice through a window at Cameron Indoor Stadium. Or a perch high above home plate at Wrigley Field, where you can see sailboats bobbing on Lake Michigan. Or stealing into Pauley Pavilion on a spring afternoon and shooting imaginary baskets in the dark. Or crammed into the crow's nest press box at Indianapolis Motor Speedway, with

Ultimately, racing is about the fans and those who savor the action on and off the track.

the Crayola cavalcade of cars rushing below.

Or, yes, maybe sitting atop a concession stand in a dusty infield.

I love stadiums full, with fans and energy and pep bands and popcorn smells—those afternoons and evenings that are an assault on all the senses. But I love them as much or more when they are empty. I love the anticipation. Or, hours later, when they are left as sole property of clean-up crews and media, I love the eerie afterglow. The day's story is still being written. Will the event live forever, or only as long as it takes the recycling crew to empty the blue bin left at the foot of your driveway?

I have come to realize that empty stadiums are actually full. If that makes any sense. They are full of ghosts. Full of history. Full of lore. Full of anticipation and afterglow and stories to survive the recycling crew.

That's what I hope this book relates. The racetracks are not merely structures. They are time capsules. This is not merely about how they look and where they were built. They are built not merely from asphalt and steel and concrete. What has made them pieces of sporting Americana is the people and events who have taken empty tracks and filled them full of stories.

—**MARK McCARTER**

Classics

Atlanta

Motor Speedway

Inaugural race:
Dixie 300, July 31, 1960

By leaning over a metal balcony rail or from a theater-type seat behind a tinted window, you can look down over the crowd.

Or, if you are of such a snobbish mind, you can look down your nose on the crowd.

If you have a friend of a friend of a friend, perhaps you can finagle an invitation to Tara Place Condominiums, a nine-story building that appears almost out of nowhere as you approach

Atlanta Motor Speedway via the winding, short-cut, two-lane country roads or clogged four-lane highway.

Other speedways have implemented luxury suites and condos. Atlanta Motor Speedway, like its cousin in Charlotte, Lowe's Motor Speedway, has mastered the idea. This is NASCAR as it appeared in the 1990s—fancy to accompany fast. This is the opulence required to cater to those who assure the sport's rich future, keeping watch over a track awash in grand history.

The million-dollar-plus units, many with six-figures' worth of interior decorating flourishes and furnishing and gizmos, are a stark contrast to the NASCAR stereotype that often plays out right across the track from the condos in the infield—say, a pair of muddy pick-ups with a tarp stretched between them serving as a make-shift tent, with barbecue smoke rising from a lip of the tent.

Tara Place Condominiums is a nine-story building that looms above the fourth turn. There are 46 units, plus a swimming pool, two tennis courts, a clubhouse and two fishing lakes. The condos have become a full-time residence for some, or a weekend get-away, or merely a place to stay and entertain in unique style a couple of weekends out of the year.

This is Atlanta Motor Speedway only in the geographic sense that the city claims most anything caught in a 50-mile net from downtown. It is well south of the Atlanta proper—official dateline of Hampton—far enough to feel remote, close enough to endure the frequent traffic nightmares of the city.

However, the speedway marched right along with the rest of Atlanta—in fact, frequently leading the parade—that was getting itself spruced up for the 1996 Summer Olympics. Despite its distance from downtown, this is an equally beautiful, functional and modern arena to its brethren in the city—Turner Field, home of

A face-lift in 1990 brought an expanded press box, luxury suites and grandstands (opposite), and the garage area, shown here during an open-wheel race, that had been sunken was built to track level.

the Braves and once the site of the Olympic opening ceremonies; Phillips Arena, home to the Hawks and Thrashers; and the Georgia Dome, the multipurpose coliseum that has hosted Super Bowls and NCAA Final Fours.

Bruton Smith bought Atlanta Motor Speedway in 1990 and began an ambitious project to modernize the place. Reportedly, more than $100 million was pumped into the project. It wasn't just condos, though their presence, as well as the myriad suites and skyboxes, provided a special and lovely touch.

Smith ordered the track to be flip-flopped, moving the back stretch to the front and vice versa. The long, straight back stretch was slightly bent to form a trioval shape as it became the front. Thousands of new grandstand seats were added there, as well as the luxury boxes and press box. A new media center was erected

in the infield.

A newer, wide pit road was built on the front side, as well as a larger, better garage area at track level. Previously, the garage area on the old front side was sunken. It was good news, bad news. The good news: Crews could watch the entire race from the pits, their views unblocked by the rows of trucks and motor homes. The bad news: Teams had to trudge up a steep ramp from the garage to the pits, a difficult task when pushing a 3,400-pound racecar or tugging an eight-foot-high toolchest with every piece of mechanical hardware imaginable.

The speedway is the best of short track racing and the best of superspeedways. It has long, sweeping turns with 24-degree banking that seemingly go on forever, giving almost the trapped-in-a-bowl sensation as Bristol. One can gauge the NASCAR handling ail-

Richard Petty's pit crew does its work on the King's car during the 1969 Dixie 500. Petty drove a Ford that season and won 10 times.

ments of "tight" and "loose" more vividly in Atlanta than almost anywhere because the cars are almost constantly in a turn, and at speeds rivaling those at Talladega and Daytona. As tires begin to give, one can follow how, lap after lap, cars begin to ease into higher and higher grooves.

Atlanta has relatively short straightaways; though it is four-tenths of a mile longer than Charlotte, its front stretch is more than 500 feet shorter. The physics of that combine for some eye-popping speeds; Geoffrey Bodine set a qualifying record of 197-plus miles per hour in 1997.

As a result, it is also one of the more dangerous tracks with a scary formula of high speeds plus constant cornering, coupled with smaller, flat, wide areas in which to avoid peril.

The speeds were pushed even higher when Atlanta welcomed the Indy Racing League in 1996, under a newly installed lighting system. Buddy Lazier, the reigning Indy 500 champ, ran the first laps in an Indy car there, and registered speeds higher than 212 mph.

Atlanta Motor Speedway held its first race in July, 1960, marking both the beginning and an end of an era.

Car racing in Atlanta had been going on since 1917, when Ralph DePalma and Barney Oldfield dueled in a match race at Lakewood Speedway, a one-mile dirt track around a lake at a resort on the outskirts of Atlanta (but long since swallowed up by the city).

Lakewood became a popular venue in the early days of stock car racing, a place for the north Georgia speed demons and moonshine runners—despite a codicil to the rules that no driver with a criminal record could race there. Perhaps appropriately, a party at Lakewood was the final destination for the heroes in one of the most famous bootlegger movies, *Smokey and the Bandit*,

Whether it was a NASCAR race or this IROC race during the 1970s, Atlanta always seemed to have empty seats. Today, with additional seating, there aren't nearly as many empty seats, though the early spring and late fall race dates sometimes lead to weather problems.

with their truckload of beer.

Though Bill Elliott is the most famous native of Dawsonville, Ga., to most NASCAR fans, a generation of drivers before him hailed from Dawsonville and spilled down Highway 9 or Highway 53—some, perhaps, with a trunk full of white lightning—toward Atlanta to do some business and do some racing. Men such as Raymond Parks, Tim Flock, Lloyd Seay and Gober Sosebee came from the north Georgia mountains and into NASCAR prominence.

And, in 1959, in the final NASCAR Winston Cup (then Grand National) event at Lakewood, a handsome lad with a beaming smile was handed his first checkered flag. Richard Petty won his first race, only to have a driver file a protest that Richard had been aided by a scoring snafu and should have been listed as the runner-up. Sure enough, the protest held up. The driver who filed

the protest: the ultimate winner, Lee Petty, Richard's dad.

With Lakewood growing obsolete, racing turned to the rolling countryside near Hampton. It often was a struggle, however. After the original owners struggled financially, Walter Nix and L.G. DeWitt purchased what was then called Atlanta International Raceway and rescued it from potential oblivion.

There was a modest 30,000-seat grandstand—now the backstretch stands—but there often were far too many empty seats. The track had too much misfortune. James Taylor, he of the hit song "Fire and Rain," should have been on retainer by Atlanta.

In 1980, the track maintenance crew hadn't been able to mow as many of the surrounding fields that served as parking lots as needed. A searing catalytic converter underneath someone's car ignited some high, dry grass. Before the blaze could be stopped, 27 vehicles were destroyed. The race was even redflagged for a while, simply to enable emergency crews in the infield to leave the track to fight the fire.

Because Atlanta's dates often fell in early spring and late fall, the weather was capricious. The late George Cunningham of *The Atlanta Constitution* used to write that "A.I.R. stood for Always It's Raining." Unless, of course, it's snowing. Which happened in March of 1993, when a massive overnight blizzard left a Christmas postcard scene, with snow blanketing the track, grandstands and team trucks that already were in the

The front straight, now the back stretch, was straight in this 1970s photo. When the track was refurbished, the back stretch became the front and was bent slightly.

garage area.

It was the still the old configuration, still a touch rustic, when Atlanta Motor Speedway was involved in one of NASCAR's most historic dates.

The Winston Cup points race was coming to a boil on November 15, 1992, at the Hooters 500.

Davey Allison, the 31-year-old youngest member of the famed "Alabama Gang," led the points race over Alan Kulwicki by 30 points and Bill Elliott by 40. Allison, son of 1983 Winston Cup champ Bobby Allison, had won 18 races since joining the Winston Cup circuit full-time in 1987. He needed

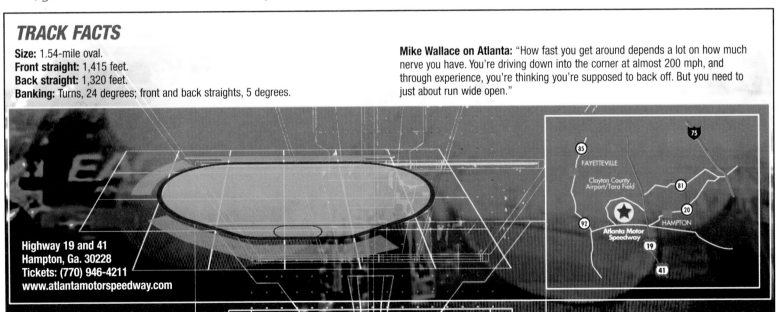

TRACK FACTS

Size: 1.54-mile oval.
Front straight: 1,415 feet.
Back straight: 1,320 feet.
Banking: Turns, 24 degrees; front and back straights, 5 degrees.

Mike Wallace on Atlanta: "How fast you get around depends a lot on how much nerve you have. You're driving down into the corner at almost 200 mph, and through experience, you're thinking you're supposed to back off. But you need to just about run wide open."

Highway 19 and 41
Hampton, Ga. 30228
Tickets: (770) 946-4211
www.atlantamotorspeedway.com

to finish sixth or better on this day to win the title over Kulwicki. Allison was, in fact, running in sixth place with less than 100 laps remaining when Ernie Irvan—who later took over Allison's ride in the No. 28 Havoline Texaco Ford—lost control because a tire was going flat. He spun in front of Allison, who T-boned Irvan's car. It knocked Allison out of the race.

Elliott and Kulwicki—a surprising title contender who symbolized his status by asking Ford if he could remove the "TH" on his car that day, so the front bumper read "UNDERBIRD"—raced much of the day in front of the field, and not far from the finish, things were left in the hands of the mathemeticians. On lap 310 of 328, Kulwicki led his 103rd lap of the race. It assured he would lead more laps than anyone else. It earned him five bonus points. When Elliott won the race and Kulwicki finished second, only 10 points separated them in the final standings, the closest finish in NASCAR history.

"Alabama Gang" loyalists shrugged off the heartbreak. Allison was, after all, so young. Few drivers of his generation, including a couple of scions of other racing families, Dale Jarrett and Sterling Marlin, had yet to show such ability and promise. And the old guard—Richard Petty, Darrell Waltrip and Harry Gant—were walking toward sunset. Allison would surely win a Winston Cup title, maybe several.

Kulwicki, meanwhile, could reign as a symbol of steadfast, stubborn independence. He was a misunderstood, almost aloof man with an engineering degree. He would leave the garage with a briefcase in the days when his peers would leave clutching a 12-ounce can. He owned this team, micromanaging it to a championship. He was the first owner-driver to win a championship

One of the most popular spots to watch racing at Atlanta, like most tracks, is from the infield caravan of motor homes.

since Richard Petty in 1979 and likely would be the last—unless he repeated.

That didn't happen. Nor did Allison win that title that seemed so assured. Within eight months, Kulwicki and Allison died, both victims of aircraft crashes. Kulwicki perished in a plane crash en route to Bristol the next April. Allison was killed in July when a helicopter he was piloting crashed in the infield at Talladega.

Despite the great sense of history that enveloped that November day at Atlanta Motor Speedway, it wasn't until subsequent events that it was revealed how much more historic the day became.

Indeed, it can be looked at as the time

Cars come out of the fourth turn and down the front straightaway during the 1967 Dixie 500.

when there was some symbolic passing of the mantel of greatness in the sport.

It was the final race for Richard Petty, the end of the extravagant "Fan Appreciation Tour" that came to a climax on the previous evening with thousands gathered at the Georgia Dome for a concert and tribute to The King. He was caught up in an accident in the race and went skidding down the front stretch, flames leaping from underneath the bright blue and red No. 43 STP Pontiac. "I went out in a blaze," Petty said. "I forgot the glory."

It also was, much more quietly, the first Winston Cup race for a skinny, baby-faced kid driver whom car owner Rick Hendrick boldly put behind the wheel.

That kid, Jeff Gordon.

During the late 1980s, Dale Earnhardt, shown running third, won three races and finished second three times at Atlanta.

FAN STAND

Bristol
Motor Speedway

Nickname:
Thunder Valley

Inaugural race:
Volunteer 500, July 30, 1961

Stand deep in that bowl on a sultry, moonlit Saturday night in August, and lean your head back a bit. Look up, up, up at the towering grandstands that encircle this place, stretching to the stars. So high up, you wonder if the patrons in the highest level seats must file a report with air-traffic control officers before excusing themselves to visit the restroom or concession stands.

Standing there is to have the sensation of being on a

narrow, big-city street, staring up at the statues blocking out the sky. It's like being at the bottom of a vast canyon with vertical walls. But don't bother to shout some rolling yodel. You couldn't hear it yourself at the moment, much less to believe your own cry would find room to echo around in the thick blanket of noise and come back to you.

Some 150,000 or so fans fill the grandstand seats that encircle the entire track, with high-falutin' sky-boxes sitting smugly at the top. With lights glowing inside them, TV monitors atwinkle with the race broadcast, the skyboxes seem a glittering tiara, perfectly crowning Bristol Motor Speedway.

It is one of NASCAR's most surprising and gratifying developments that Bristol has become one of the sport's crown jewels. This old dairy farm at the base of a hollow in northeast Tennessee provides a unique race and unique experience. TV ratings are sky-

With Bristol's short (.533-mile), banked track that virtually ensures non-stop, fender-to-fender and door-to-door action from the front of the field to the back—and lighting to illuminate a Saturday night race for 150,000-plus faithful—the atmosphere at "Thunder Valley" is like none other on the Winston Cup circuit.

high. Sellouts are the norm. For the late-summer Saturday night race, tickets are as treasured as a patron's badge to The Masters, a courtside seat at the Final Four.

Ed Clark, the president of Atlanta Motor Speedway, one of Bristol's cousins in the Bruton Smith racetrack empire, was deep in that Bristol bowl one August afternoon before the evening's bedlam began. He was as amazed and mystified as anyone—and more than a little envious.

"It's a cult," Clark said. "It has created itself. It's nothing we have done."

Bristol Motor Speedway—"Thunder Valley", they call it—often is referred to as a racing equivalent to some Barnum & Bailey three-ring circus. But that's selling it three or four rings short. It's impossible to follow all the action.

There are four steeply-banked corners, at 36 degrees, the most dramatic banking anywhere on the Winston Cup circuit. They are

constant conflicts with the laws of physics and centrifugal force; tires are tested to the max as they grip the concrete and prevent—most of the time—cars from flinging themselves into the walls.

The straightaways, barely the length of a couple of football fields laid end zone to end zone, are constantly full of cars dicing and banging. To merely follow the leading cars as they sprint and slide and steer is to cheat yourself. Typically, the best action is in the middle of the pack.

Then, inside the whole maelstorm, there is the infield, and the two pit roads. Invariably, there is a wounded car coming in for first-aid, or perhaps jacked up behind the pit wall, undergoing radical surgery underneath the glow of halogen spotlights while frantic crewmen scurry about glum-faced and determined like emergency room personnel.

When it comes time for the inevitable eight or 10 or 12 yellow-flag stops, the close quarters on pit road lend an air of danger and excitement.

At .533 miles, it is NASCAR's second-shortest track, next to Mar-

The tight quarters at Bristol usually lead to a lot of incidents on the track, especially in the corners, and consequent yellow flags. This wreck during the Food City 500 in the late 1990s included Mike Skinner (31), Chad Little (97) and Bobby Labonte (18).

tinsville. But unlike the relatively flat Martinsville track, Bristol's banking provides more the sense of a velodrome, "like being thrown around in a wild, violent carnival ride for four hours at a time," Dale Earnhardt Jr. said. "I've compared it to flying a jet fighter around the inside of a basketball arena," Mark Martin said.

The straightaways are long enough for some quick bursts of speed, especially when a driver can take some momentum out of a corner. The strategy is then to dive as low and hard as possible into a corner, keeping the preferred inside line. Then, to accelerate coming out of the corner and get a good, clean, fast line down the straightaway.

It's pretty much like the shampoo instructions: Shampoo. Rinse. Repeat. Accelerate. Dive. Accelerate. Repeat. Twice a lap, 500 laps a race.

Of course, the chances of a good, clean, fast line are rare. The string of traffic is too long. There generally is a car on the inside or outside. Or both.

Bristol's track is 40 feet wide. Some simple math says that there are some 112,569 square feet of racing room. Fill it full of 43 race cars, about 4,300 square feet of automobile, and that leaves 108,269 square feet of empty space.

The question: Where is it?

You'd never get a driver to believe there is that much open room. Nor can you conceive that while watching, whether from

It's not the easiest racetrack to get to—it's nestled in a hollow in northeast Tennessee—but thousands upon thousands do it twice a year, to watch the trucks roll into town, to watch the racing and to check out the latest memorabilia featuring their favorite drivers.

the upper reaches, or down so close you'll have to floss tire rubber from your teeth the next morning, or down in the bowl, looking up at those mesmerized cult members

Bristol makes the racing purists zip their lips. You know the ones. The fans who grow adamant and defensive and sanctimoniously preach that people don't watch racing for the wrecks.

People watch Bristol for the wrecks.

Or at least for the sparks flying, the paint trading, the flames exploding out

of headers, the metal grinding. It is a short track, with even shorter tempers. Seldom a race goes by that some wrecked driver doesn't fling equipment or obscene gestures or insults to another driver who snowplowed him out of the way.

"It's not racing," some complain. There isn't enough room. It's more physical than it should be. It's bumper cars. It's like watching a snake trying to swallow its own tail, the way things are stretched out, single-file, all the way around.

To the contrary, it is racin' the way it used to be. It is Saturday night under the lights, beating and banging and letting human skill and guts and guile determine a winner, instead of who has the best space-age, overgrown science project straight from a wind tunnel. Racing purists have to accept it: Bristol is pure racing.

And pure racing packs the place.

Seven hours before a race, you can't find a piece of right-of-way alongside Highway 11 for a mile either direction where

Here's how Mark Martin describes driving Bristol: "I've compared it to flying a jet fighter around the inside of a basketball arena."

someone hasn't set up camp, with coolers emptying, grills sizzling and parties raging. So abundant are the spectators, and their parking and tailgating locations so widespread, Bristol officials eventually implemented a rule for safety: No vehicular traffic may move for 45 minutes after the checkered flag. That lets pedestrians reach their cars without being endangered.

Wait too long to make hotel reservations and you'll be staying in Asheville or Knoxville, two hours away. Locals have even taken

TRACK FACTS

Size: .533-mile oval.
Front straight: 650 feet.
Back straight: 650 feet.
Banking: Turns, 36 degrees; front and back straights, 16 degrees.

John Andretti on Bristol: "Guys beat and bang here, and you've got to be lucky to get through all that to have a good finish. It can get real ugly here, and it can get ugly in a hurry. The guy who did the concrete here, I certainly wouldn't have him do my driveway."

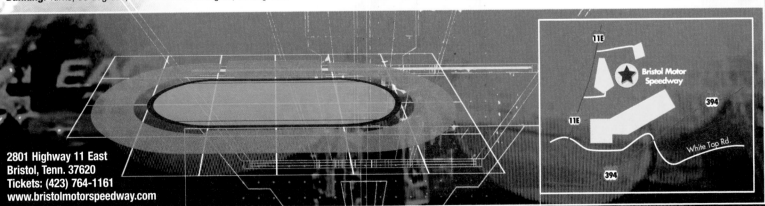

2801 Highway 11 East
Bristol, Tenn. 37620
Tickets: (423) 764-1161
www.bristolmotorspeedway.com

*Racing came to Bristol in
the summer of 1961 ...*

to renting out spare bedrooms, or their entire houses, to Thunder Valley addicts.

Originally, the track essentially was a miniature version of Charlotte Motor Speedway. Track developers Larry Carrier, Carl Moore and R.G. Pope merely wanted something a little more intimate. They began construction in 1960 south of Bristol, a cozy little town bisected by the Tennessee-Virginia state line.

The first NASCAR event was held July 30, 1961, with seating for 18,000—about a tenth of the current attendance. After a 17-year-old rising Nashville star named Brenda Lee sang the national anthem, Jack Smith, with relief help from Johnny Allen, won the race. Only 19 of 42 cars survived the 500 laps.

It cost a reported $600,000 to purchase the land and build the Bristol track, sitting alongside Highway 11. In 1969, the track was reshaped from the half-mile originally designed, and the banks carved out at the present 36 degrees. In August 1992, it was the first all-concrete speedway to host a Winston Cup race. Darrell Waltrip won that event, the last of his record 12 Bristol wins, and the next-to-last of his 84 career triumphs.

In 1996, after three ownership changes and having taken possession of the speedway and its debts 11 years earlier, Carrier sold Bristol Motor Speedway to racing impressario Bruton Smith for $26 million. There were a reported $50 million in improvements made over the next six years.

... its 36-degree banking took shape in 1969, bringing about a short track with even shorter tempers. Bristol is considered by many as pure racing that requires guts and skill to win.

Smith also invested millions back into the adjacent Bristol Dragway, which was temporarily closed in 1997 to permit a $15 million improvements project that included a four-story tower and 24 luxury suites.

Sometimes, when you stand deep in that bowl and look up, up, up over the grandstands, there is a full moon. In fact, it seems as if there always is a full moon, or should be, at Bristol, such are the wild events. Fantastic finishes are the norm.

There was 1995, when Dale Earnhardt bumped Terry Labonte on the last lap. Labonte still won, sliding backward across the line. Four years later, after Waltrip had already spun Labonte out once, Earnhardt got him again. This time, the "bump-and-run" left things open for Earnhardt to win. Said Earnhardt, grinning, "I stir up controversy, don't I?"

In 2002, a driver who steers far from controversy had his turn. Jeff Gordon, who was in the thralls of a 31-race winless streak, pulled a bump-and-run on Rusty Wallace on the final lap.

As relatively minor as those incidents were, Bristol has seen some spectacular crashes.

In practice for the 1988 Busch 500, Wallace blew a tire on the front stretch, causing his car to barrel-roll down the track. It sent Wallace to the hospital overnight and necessitated a relief driver, Larry Pearson, during the race. Wallace and Pearson combined to finish ninth. It knocked Rusty out of first place in the Winston Cup

point standings, and he never regained the lead.

In 1990, Michael Waltrip hit the turn 2 access gate and his car virtually disintegrated. Miraculously, he was unharmed and drove in the Winston Cup race the next day. In August 2002, Mike Harmon mirrored that wreck. Says Waltrip, "It was exactly my crash. I was a little bit groggy and slow to get out of my car when I had the wreck that day. I'll be darned if Mike didn't just jump right out and was standing there. I told him, 'Get ready because you'll laugh about this the rest of your life.' Because people come up to me all the time and laugh about the deal at Bristol."

Years ago, this speedway captured the fancy and imagination of a sturdy Bristol lad whose father, Orville, would drive him by the track to follow its construction. The kid was 5, maybe 6 years old. And he already was falling in love.

"When it opened up and it had racecars on it, I thought that was the slickest thing since peanut butter," the lad recalls now. When the racing began, "We paid a farmer a couple of bucks for a whole carload of us to sit there on the edge and watch the race," he says.

He later began working in one of the track concession stands, cooking and selling hamburgers and hot dogs. It was his first job in automobile racing. As time went on, that youngster, Mike Helton, moved considerably higher up the ladder. In November 2000, he became the president of NASCAR.

Before Helton moved from Bristol and got into the business of racing, he worked at a local radio station. He hosted a sports show, and worked as a sports reporter. Among his duties was to cover the Bristol races. Helton's old station's call letters seem now so perfectly appropriate to the speedway's growth. It was WOPI radio, an acronym for "Watch Our Popularity Increase."

The confined quarters of the infield and bowl-shaped stands that stretch to the sky give Bristol the feel of a three-ring circus as much as a racetrack.

Darlington
Raceway

Nickname:
The Lady in Black

Inaugural race:
Southern 500, September 4, 1950

More than one crew chief has pondered this simple advice for a rookie driver at Darlington:

"Go on out there now, before you even take a full lap, and slap the wall. Just get it over with right off the bat."

"The Darlington Stripe" is a tattoo that all cars eventually have applied here from hitting the wall. It is as inevitable for a racecar driver as a torn ACL is for a running back, a tender elbow is for a pitcher, a spot

Darlington has retained its classic appeal after more than a half century of racing. In 1957, the date of this race, the grandstands were smaller and the cars slower, but the racing was as challenging as it is today on the speedway that has been labeled The Track Too Tough to Tame.

below Tiger Woods on the leaderboard for a golfer.

The "Stripe" is a scar of smeared paint somewhere along the right side. It frequently is accompanied by a wrinkled fender or scraped quarterpanel or a rear bumper left dangling, like some loose string on a sweater you're hesitant to tug, lest the whole thing come unraveled.

It is a fair exchange of paint. The drivers are making their mark on Darlington as well, like spray-paint grafitti on a subway car. Angry swipes of black tire rubber and whatever flavors of Crayola that decorate the car are left behind. The outside wall, freshly painted a virginal white each day before a race, becomes a work

of abstract art by day's end. It's as smudged and smeared as Tammy Fay Bakker's makeup after a day-long crying jag.

"The Darlington Stripe" is but one signature for Darlington Raceway, this magnificent, 1.33-mile icon in the center of South Carolina.

This speedway is awash in history. It was NASCAR's first fully-paved track and held its first race in 1950. Despite modern touches, it still feels old. With all of the generic, vanilla new tracks, having a classic is not a bad thing.

Darlington is a visit to the attic in your grandmother's house in the country. It's a classic Bogart movie in black and white. It shouldn't smell like burning rubber and race fuel. It should smell like a cedar chest full of yellowing newspapers and scrapbooks full of crinkling black-and-white family photos.

As Jeff Burton once said, "It's nice to go somewhere where the stuff doesn't look all fancy and cool like all the other racetracks. And I think that's OK."

This was a place where they used to race convertibles. Where the greatest names in NASCAR figuratively and literally earned their stripes. Where the track is so imposing it gets two nicknames: "The Lady in Black" and "The Track Too Tough to Tame." Where, more than any speedway on the circuit, you sense the ghosts of the past.

Maybe Hollywood is to blame. Seems that every 1960s and 1970s hokey racing movie—is that redundant?—had some scene of cars sailing into and flying over the metal guard rails on the outside of one of Darlington's banked turns.

Darlington always draws comparisons to old venues in other sports. Fenway Park, Yankee Stadium and Wrigley Field come to mind. And not so much for the sense of history but the quirky dimensions. Old major league stadiums often were configured into odd shapes because of the various obstacles of the city. Darlington was made quirky because of the obstacles of the country.

The obstacle was named "Ramsey's Pond."

Harold Brasington, a farmer and construction magnate, had been a racer and was a friend of Bill France Sr. As NASCAR was in its infancy, Brasington envisioned a paved track in South Carolina. He had visited Indianapolis and was mesmerized by that speedway. He wanted a similar venue here in what South Carolinians

Drivers need some luck to survive 500 miles at The Lady in Black, and some, including Fred Lorenzen, have tried to buoy their chances.

know as the "PeeDee" region

Brasington found an appropriate piece of land. It was a peanut farm, belonging to a man named J.S. Ramsey. Brasington acquired the land from Ramsey; local lore says he acquired it by holding a better hand in a game of poker. Whatever the case, Brasington conceded to one of Ramsey's requests—that he leave intact the minnow pond on the farm.

In doing so, it necessitated the track's unique egg shape, as synonymous with Darlington as the Stripe.

In 1997, they scrambled the egg.

Darlington needed more seats. But the Colvin Grandstand on the front stretch, which had lost much of its familiar overhang roof in a 1989 hurricane, couldn't be expanded. Brasington had managed to design his track to avoid the minnow pond, but he also put it too closely to Harry Byrd Highway (South Carolina 34 & 151). The Colvin Grandstand had no room behind it for the necessary foundation and framework to enlarge it.

There was, however, plenty of room on the backstretch, where concrete bleachers provided cheap-seat opportunities for fans who didn't mind the sunburns and inevitable layer of tire rubber they'd wear home, looking like blistering chimney-sweeps, from the track.

It was decided to flip-flop the track. The mammoth Tyler Tower grandstand was erected on the back stretch. In 1997, the start-finish line was put on the back stretch. What was once Turn 1 became Turn 3. Unlike the reconfiguration at Atlanta, which turned that symetrical oval into a tri-oval, the integrity of the Darlington Raceway remained the same.

In 1997, the front and back stretches were flip-flopped because the back stretch was the only place to add seats.

The pit crew strategy at Darlington, whether it's 2000 (above) or 1964 (right): Change tires, clear the debris front the front grille, add fuel and reassure your driver that every other driver is as miserable and uncomfortable as he.

Don't mess with imperfection.

Darlington produced arguably the greatest press box vantage point in sports. It sits above the entrance to the old Turn 1. With a sort of eerie IMAX movie feel to it, cars appeared headed straight at reporters as drivers sped down the long, wide front stretch, making the left turn directly underneath. Veteran scribes recall the day when the Darlington press box, smaller and even more rustic, was not even enclosed. Track P.R. officials passed out goggles to the writers to protect their eyes from the tire rubber, leaving the reporters raccoon-eyed at day's end.

Because of the wacky shape of this place, each turn is a challenge. Elsewhere, drivers at least can settle into something of a pattern. Each entrance and exit are at least similar, if not identi-cal. Not here. Though the straights are alike—1,229 feet, and a forgiving 90 feet wide—each leads into a narrower chute that must have the feel of going from a wide-open ski hill and feeding into a bobsled run.

Turns 1 and 2—the wide end—are banked at 25 degrees. The track is 79 feet wide at this end. The radius of the turn is a more sweeping 600 degrees.

Turns 3 and 4 are slightly less banked, at 23 degrees, and the track is only 62 feet wide. The radius is a much tighter 525 degrees.

Few drivers concern themselves with the inside line. Old films of Richard Petty and David Pearson and that generation show drivers all but hugging the outside wall all the way around. Two keys are

to come off the wall efficiently out of Turn 2 for a good run down the back, and to avoid trouble coming off Turn 4. One bobble, and it's easy to slap the wall on the entrance to the back stretch, next to a crossover gate. Not that anyone in NASCAR might try to circumvent the rulebook, but there are stories of cars with springs placed inside the right rear fender between the body and framework that enabled a driver to hit the wall here and bounce away without caving in the car's wheelwell or bending the A-frame.

The racing groove moves gradually higher and higher as the race goes on. This is a rough track, with too much beach sand whipped up and plopped here by too many tropical storms along the Atlantic Coast, just 75 miles to the southeast. That gnaws away tires, and cars begin to grow looser, sliding higher. Gnawed tires lead to those overgrown eraser-shavings of rubber that clog grilles.

The priority level on a Darlington pit stop:

(1) Change tires.

TRACK FACTS

Size: 1.366-mile oval.
Front straight: 1,229 feet.
Back straight: 1,229 feet.
Banking: Turns 1 and 2, 25 degrees; Turns 3 and 4, 23 degrees; front straight, 3 degrees; back straight, 2 degrees.

Ward Burton on Darlington: "It's very much a handling racetrack. Any time you lose concentration or hit something on the track, like some oil just a little bit, you can get into the wall in a hurry."

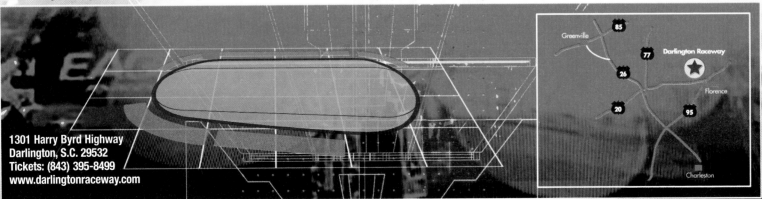

1301 Harry Byrd Highway
Darlington, S.C. 29532
Tickets: (843) 395-8499
www.darlingtonraceway.com

(2) Brush away the gunk on the grilles that blocks air flow and causes oil and water temperatures to rise into the boiling zone.

(3) Add fuel. And, perhaps,

(4) Reassure the driver that the other 42 drivers are just as miserable and worn-out as he.

"The place is so tricky there isn't a perfect place to be," Kyle Petty says. "Probably the best place to be is in the lead two laps after a restart. That way you are in front of everybody else, and the only mistakes you have to worry about are your own. Any place else at Darlington is the worst place to be. You hear 'Race the racetrack; race the racetrack,' and that is pretty much the case a lot of the time. But it goes further than that. You're not only racing the racetrack, you have to race and dodge all of the guys who forgot to race the racetrack."

"That's a racetrack where we have to be so careful where we pass," Bobby Hamilton says. "It is a driver's racetrack for sure. It's a place that's been known to bite a driver. She's finicky but tolerable in you know where and when to push yourself out there."

Brasington's vision was tremendously crowded. And still over-

Coming out of Turn 4 clean is a key at Darlington because the racing groove is high on the track, dangerously close to the wall.

whelmingly influenced by Indianapolis.

When they lined up September 4, 1950, for the Southern 500, the inaugural race here, Brasington had the cars lined up three-across for the start. Just like Indy.

Except, unlike Indy's 11 rows of three, Brasington had 25 rows of three. An incredible 75 cars began that race. Johnny Mantz, driving a Plymouth co-owned by Bill France, Curtis Turner and others, won the race. Earlier in the week, race promoters had been using the same car to run errands around town.

Mantz's team had a secret. It installed truck tires on the car, which handled the wear and tear much better than tires from passenger cars. Even then, tire wear was the Darlington X factor.

Old drivers will tell you, in the tone of a parent recounting that daily 5-mile hike to school through blinding snow-storms, of afternoons when tires wore out rapidly in the early days of Darling-ton. Crew members, so legend goes, left the track, jacked up their street cars and surrendered their own tires to the racing effort.

Other legends were created in the infield. This is where they first allowed fans to camp in the infield, creating the Woodstock-

In 1992, the rains came and cut short the race, and Darrell Waltrip (right) was declared the winner. Davey Allison, who was leading at halfway, pitted shortly before the rain and wound up fifth, losing ground in the points race and a chance to win the Winston Million bonus.

for-good-ol'-boys tradition that still thrives.

NASCAR's most historic track was not be kind to the sport's winningest driver. Richard Petty had only three wins here. Instead, it became the province of a pair of locals guys. Cale Yarborough, from Timmonsville, a mere 15 miles away, used to sneak into the track. And security guards used to bounce him right out. But there was nothing they could do when he got behind the wheel. Yarborough won five Darlington events.

David Pearson, from Spartanburg, some 180 miles down the road, always was acknowledged by Petty as "the best driver I ever raced against." Pearson earned some of that respect here, with 10 Darlington triumphs, more than anyone else as the new millennium arrived.

Those 10 wins didn't make Pearson as much money all together as Bill Elliott collected in one day here. In 1985, "Awesome Bill" collected the first "Winston Million," a bonus given to any driver who won three of the "Big Four"—the Daytona 500, Winston 500 at Talladega, Coca-Cola 600 at Charlotte and Southern 500 at Darlington.

Alas, Darlington has had to stave off constant rumors of its impending demise, or at least losing one of its annual races. Darlington, a pretty, sleepy town of barely more than 6,000, and nearby Florence are in an area already saturated with NASCAR events, drawing from the same fan base as Charlotte and Rockingham. Though expansion in the 1990s doubled the seating capacity, it still can't match the size—or, more important—luxuries of newer tracks.

And, oh yes, by the way:

Not far from the road that leads into the track via the Turn 1 tunnel, behind the Pearson Tower that looms over the skinny end of the egg, is Ramsey's Pond.

Daytona

International Speedway

Nickname:
World Center of Racing

Inaugural Race:
Daytona 500, February 22, 1959

It's a seven-mile drive from the beach. Or, in another perspective, it's a million miles from the beach.

Daytona International Speedway is NASCAR's home, its mecca, its nerve center. It seems to be the world's largest erector-set creation, a long, towering construction of steel and concrete dominating the landscape along Speedway Boulevard, just off the Interstate 95 ribbon that ties Maine to Miami.

This is NASCAR's Mother Ship, the home of the sport's business operation. It is the grandest, proudest speedway. This is a place redolent in history and, considering the season traditionally opens here, with much curious anticipation of the future.

It is synonymous with NASCAR. It is not the circuit's most opulent speedway by any means. Nor does it have the history of Darlington or that relative newcomer to the NASCAR universe, Indianapolis Motor Speedway. Nor does it quite provide the electrifying speed of its clone in the Alabama countryside, Talladega. Nor—with deepest, most humble apologies to the surf, sand, sun and seafood—is Daytona any longer the most seductive destination on the circuit for fans, sponsors and platinum-level credit card holders, not with Las Vegas now part of the club.

Daytona is simply a most perfect amalgam of them all. If Bristol is NASCAR's answer to Wrigley Field's friendly confines and Darlington is quirky, asymetrical Fenway Park, then Daytona is its Yankee Stadium. Daytona is mammoth, in breadth and length and height. Grandstands tower 10 stories high

on the front stretch. Banners gloriously hang from each, boasting the names of the drivers for whom various seating sections are named. At 2.5 miles in circumference, Daytona is longer than every oval-style speedway in NASCAR except Talladega.

Daytona is a competitive track that demands the most from driver and machine. It requires the steel nerves for white-knuckle, close-quarter drafting, the ability to run lap after lap

The first race at the Daytona International Speedway was held in 1959, and the winner was Lee Petty. The track's unique trioval layout allowed spectators to view racing all around the track despite its 2.5-mile length.

after lap mere inches from the nearest car while going upward of 190 miles per hour. It also requires the mechanical expertise to concoct the perfect setup to manuever corners that are nowhere near as benign as they seem.

It symbolic with NASCAR's evolution. It was built to replace the most fundamental and elementary form of racing: man's need to go as fast as possible in a straight line. That's what the post-World War II speed demons were doing in Daytona, exploding down the beach with deafening roars and cars shaking spasmodically. Eventually, racing outgrew the beach, necessitating the construction of the speedway. The old days still are

memorialized to an extent; the beach is open to automobile traffic in many stretches, often an endless line of SUVs, four-wheel-drive trucks and convertibles that seem to be loud, vibrating boom boxes on wheels.

The traffic is especially thick come February, when that I-95 ribbon pours forth hundreds of thousands of visitors for the annual Daytona 500. It is a festival, a reunion, a long-awaited answer and, likely as not, another page of history waiting to be written.

NASCAR runs backward. It holds its version of the Super Bowl first, with all the incumbent hype, hoopla and media hordes.

Then it plays its season. The Daytona 500 opens the year, bringing the sport back together in the unpredictably fickle weather—pack sweaters and jackets, swimsuits and sunscreen—of Florida Februarys. It ends the brief two-month hibernation during which teams reload, rebuild and re-energize for the long haul ahead. It is the time of fresh, buoyant optimism if you are a racer, when you haven't blown an engine, fender-slapped a wall or finished a lap down—and when you think your car will fly gracefully with wings of limitless speed and efficiency. "The Great American Race," as TV breathlessly promotes it, can crush that optimism or fill it with even more helium. And as history proves, it plays no favorites. It took Dale Earnhardt 20 times to win a Daytona 500, and 17 times for Darrell Waltrip.

It introduces old drivers in new cars and new drivers in old cars. It welcomes new sponsors. It confuses with number changes. Invariably, broadcasters are so accustomed to a certain driver in a certain car, they flub their calls, like a flustered parent sputtering the names of all the offspring before getting around to the right one. Surely, with the myriad off-season changes, souvenir program sales at Daytona must be double what they are anywhere else.

Journalists who will see no other race all season will be here. The garage area and pits and grandstands are thick with spectators in identical shirts and/or caps, VIPs being coddled and entertained with a long weekend of racing and golf and beach time by the corporate monoliths who fuel the sport with

Ward Burton celebrates his Daytona 500 win in 2002 amidst the media crush.

Long before the speedway was built, racing went back to as far as 1903 on the hard-packed sand of Ormond Beach, north of the Daytona Beach strip.

the financial support. The stands are full of loyalists who likely as not made their hotel reservations the day they checked out after the previous year's race, their faces glowing red with sun and wind.

The speedway is the hub of development, sitting among an array of motels, shopping centers, car dealerships and restaurants that provide race fans such essentials as chicken wings and cold beer and, advertised by that seductive green and red neon sign, "Hot Doughnuts Now." The Daytona Beach Kennel Club, for greyhound racing, sits at its right elbow. Greyhounds, it seems, are about the only things not to race at Daytona Inter-

national Speedway. Though the Daytona 500 is its most luminous event, the track also is the site of motorcycle, go-kart and truck races and a 24-hour sports car event, all wrapped up in a monthlong extravaganza called "Speedweeks."

The speedway became truly luminous itself in 1998, hosting its first nighttime Winston Cup event after a $5 million project made Daytona the largest lighted sports arena in the world. With 1,835 lights, Musco Lighting, the contractor, said the lighting was equivalent to standard residential lights of 24,285 city blocks. Alas, the celebration of light was postponed. Because of raging wildfires across the breadth of the Florida peninsula in

July 1998, the Pepsi 400 was postponed until October 17.

Though NASCAR's growth has necessitated several offices and operations in other cities, the headquarters are in Daytona Beach, along with the offices of International Speedway Corporation. Daytona USA, an interactive museum, sits on the speedway grounds. Annually, Daytona USA commits an egregious act of kidnapping: The winning car at the Daytona 500 is confiscated and put on display in the museum for a year, not always to the delight of the car's driver

In addition to playing host to the biggest race of the season, Daytona houses NASCAR headquarters and Daytona USA, an interactive museum.

and team.

It was in Daytona Beach where a mechanic named Bill France Sr. settled—but only through fate. He was moving his young family from Washington to Miami for warmer weather in 1935 when his car broke down in Daytona. He decided to stay, especially after learning of the area's racing heritage.

Since 1903, cars had raced on the hard-packed sand of Ormond Beach, north of the Daytona Beach "strip." France began promoting some of those races and by 1947, began build-

---

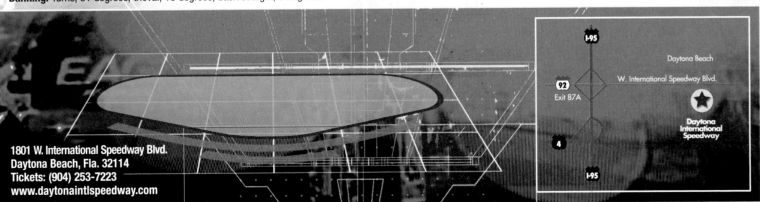

TRACK FACTS

Size: 2.5-mile trioval.
Front straight: 1,900-feet chutes to and from the trioval.
Back straight: 3,000 feet.
Banking: Turns, 31 degrees; trioval, 18 degrees; back straight, 3 degrees.

Rusty Wallace on Daytona: "Do I enjoy being out there for 200 laps, side by side, can't even breathe or blink? I don't enjoy that. But it's the way we race here now."

1801 W. International Speedway Blvd.
Daytona Beach, Fla. 32114
Tickets: (904) 253-7223
www.daytonaintlspeedway.com

I-95
92
Exit 87A
Daytona Beach
W. International Speedway Blvd.
4
Daytona International Speedway
I-95

ing the foundation for NASCAR. Other asphalt speedways already were in operation as venues for this fledgling circuit, notably the oval at Darlington. When France decided to move his races from the beach where the booming development and increasing traffic had made it unfeasible to race—and collect the spectators' money!—he wanted to assure his track was the biggest and best.

For $3 million, he built Daytona International Speedway, a 2.5-mile high-banked circuit in the much-imitated trioval shape. That was a deal for the customers. By forming a slight V in the stands and having a subtle bend in the front stretch, fans wouldn't have to lean forward to see past their neighbors to see cars headed their direction. The track even has its own lake, a 44-acre rectangular body of water running parallel to the backstretch called Lake Lloyd.

Grandstands wrapped nearly halfway around the speedway by the 1990s, including stands on the distant, back part of the track ingeniously marketed as the "Superstretch," and constant improvements are made. But the fact that Daytona International Speedway

has had few dramatic face-lifts is testament to Big Bill France's wisdom and prescience.

The first race here was February 22, 1959, and was won by Lee Petty in a virtual dead heat with Tim Beauchamp in a field of 53 cars. It took several days, after photos were reviewed many times, before Petty, in a $2,500 Oldsmobile, was declared the winner.

But it was his son, Richard Petty, who would be more inexorably tied to Daytona. "King Richard" won the first of his seven Daytona 500s in 1964. But it was his 1979 win that was a watershed moment for NASCAR. It was the first time CBS aired a race start to finish; previously racing was tape-delayed and heavily edited. Much of the East Coast was snowed in so, as Petty later said, "We had a captive audience." And, before it ended, a captivated audience.

Petty trailed Donnie Allison and Cale Yarborough on the final lap when Allison and Yarborough collided on the backstretch. As they spun out, coming to rest only a few feet apart in the infield grass, Petty cruised to the checkered flag.

Classic moments at Daytona: Richard Petty (opposite) drives to victory in the 1974 Daytona 500. In the 1979 race, a scuffle broke out among Cale Yarborough (right), Donnie Allison (left) and Donnie's brother, Bobby. Cale's and Donnie's final-lap crash allowed Petty to slip by for the win.

Then, suddenly, the TV cameras caught a fracas on the infield. Bobby Allison galloped to the rescue of his brother. Yarborough gamely fought off both brothers. As Bobby Allison wryly said later, "He went to beating on my fist with his nose."

The last of Petty's 200 NASCAR wins came at Daytona on July 4, 1984. President Ronald Reagan decided to attend the race; it was, after all, an election year. Flying south on Air Force One, he gave the "Gentlemen, start your engines!" orders. He landed at the Daytona airport, directly behind the speedway as the race was in progress. At age 47, Petty beat Yarborough on a sprint to the start-finish line, after a caution with two laps remaining, to sew up the win.

Daytona forever could lay claim to being the only racetrack to celebrate both a president and a King on the same day.

For this generation and generations to come, Daytona also will be known as the site of one of NASCAR's darkest days. It was February 18, 2001. On the final turn of the final lap, Dale Earnhardt's No. 3 GM Goodwrench Chevrolet suddenly veered up the track and into the outside wall at 180 mph. He was killed instantly.

Earnhardt had become as synonymous with Daytona as Petty had been the previous era. Earnhardt won 34 races at Daytona, including 12 Twin 125 qualifying races, six IROC races and seven Busch Grand National events. Ironically, the Daytona 500 kept eluding him. Misfortune after misfortune cost him, including a blown tire

One of the unfortunate, enduring images that Daytona provides is the fourth-turn wall where seven-time Winston Cup champion Dale Earnhardt crashed and died in the 2001 Daytona 500.

in Turn 3 on the last lap in 1990, handing the win to an unknown named Derrike Cope.

Finally, on February 15, 1998, Earnhardt held off Bobby Labonte to win the Daytona 500. In an economy of words that said volumes, Earnhardt's crew chief, Larry McReynolds proclaimed it "dadgum special."

Three years and three days later, Earnhardt was killed on this very track. As Earnhardt crashed, Michael Waltrip was driving an Earnhardt-owned car to his first Winston Cup victory; Dale Earnhardt Jr. was the runner-up.

On the morning after the crash, bouquets of flowers were poking through the holes of the chain-link fence at Gate 8, at the base of a steep, grassy bank outside the speedway. At the top of the bank was a gray-white concrete wall. Right above Gate 8 was the spot where Earnhardt hit the wall at that fatally awkward angle.

Among notes of mourning and condolence and tribute attached to the fence was as an official-looking document. It was an American Kennel Club registration certificate, issued to a Rick Grenawalt of Holly Hill, Fla.

It was the registration of a purebred dog born on November 11, 1999. It was named "Master Earnhardt of Daytona."

It was no surprise if you ever had watched his namesake race to learn that Master Earnhardt was a black Rottweiler.

Indianapol

Motor Speedway

Nickname:
The Brickyard

Inaugural race:
Indianapolis 500, May 30, 1911

For some, it is the scoring pylon, that tall, spindly scoreboard with the running order, 1 through 33, the round, white lights like dots on dominoes. It stands at the start-finish line, its head poking even higher into the sky than the grandstands across the way.

For others, it is the yard of bricks, the ribbon bisecting the pavement from the outside wall to pit road, serving as the start-finish line. More important, it

The pace car (white) is at the head of the field before the start of the 1916 Indianapolis 500, which was won by Dario Resta.

The field takes the green flag for the start of the 1959 Indianapolis 500, which was won by Rodger Ward. Three years later, Ward again drove to victory in the 500.

serves as a symbol, a reminder that, once upon a time, this whole place was indeed a yard of teeth-rattling, suspension-mangling bricks.

For others, it is the simple sign that reads "Gasoline Alley," stretching above the garage area and hinting of mechanical mysteries and miracles beyond.

Maybe it's a mental slide-show of beaming drivers, each wearing a laurel around his neck and guzzling from a jar of milk. Or it's Jim Nabors warbling "Back Home Again in Indiana," or any of the other pageantry that accompanies racing's most famous day.

Maybe it's the narrow tunnel that always seems to be in shad-

ows, the track's front stretch running endlessly past the covered grandstand on the outside, with pit road and the bleachers and buildings of the infield on the other. If you're inside a racecar at full speed for the first time in that tunnel, "It's like, 'Whoa!'"

So says an Indiana kid who should know. Name of Jeff Gordon.

The indelible images and memories vary from person to person. After all, Indianapolis Motor Speedway is more than a mere oval racetrack. It is a tableau of history. It is a bit of American heritage, a Mt. Rushmore or Old Ironsides for the sporting set.

Even its logo oozes history, especially compared with the funky, computerized, Disney-fied creations of current day. It is a pair of

wings, as if plucked from Mercury, the god of speed, encircled by a tire. From the tire blossoms a spray of colorful racing flags.

Aside from Yankee Stadium, there might be no more famous sporting venue in the country. With 250,000 seats, plus the wide-open spaces of the infield, it is the country's largest arena—and one of the oldest. The first Indianapolis 500 was held in 1911. There has been racing at Indy longer than at Daytona and Darlington speedways put together. For all of NASCAR's domination of the racing marketplace at the end of the 20th century, Indy remained synonymous with speed, and the Indy 500 continued as a Memorial Day tradition.

As humongous as the place is, the speedway almost sneaks up on you as you approach on Crawfordsville Road to the west—or it would if every other business didn't have "Speedway" in its name. The grandstands are low, and the track is sandwiched by neighborhoods and businesses and industries. To have a true sense of size, pull into the main gate on 16th Street. Duck under the track through the tunnel and emerge nearly at the front steps of the handsome Speedway Hall of Fame Museum.

The museum holds some 75 cars of varying vintages, as well as photos and other memorabilia from Indy races. It's a living monument to the evolution of racing automobiles, from those resembling beer kegs attached to skinny tires to those with pterodactyl wings to the sleek wedges that are today's Indy cars.

"Racing Capital of the World," it says on the building's facade. It's hard to argue that after a visit inside.

A bus shuttles visitors around the track. Here's what they'll traverse.

Each of the turns is a quarter-mile in length. Turns 1 and 2 are connected by a one-eighths mile short chute; ditto Turns 3 and 4. The turns are banked almost imperceptibly, at 9 degrees. The

Two of the traditions of Indianapolis Motor Speedway are Gasoline Alley (left), and the yard of bricks that remains to mark the start-finish line. Bill Elliott, with his son Chase watching, and members of the Dodge No. 9 team kiss the bricks during a ceremony following Elliott's win in the Brickyard 400 in 2002.

straights are five-eighths of a mile each. It is perfectly symmetrical, an oval with square shoulders at each end.

It is a wide track—50 feet on the straights, 60 feet in the turns —so that the three-wide IndyCar starts are not so claustrophobic. With their spidery suspension and light weight—IndyCars are but 1,620 pounds—they corner Indy as if on rails.

Because Winston Cup cars are 8 inches longer and 1,780 pounds heavier, NASCAR's machines don't corner nearly as well here because the corners are so flat. Because they tip-toe through the turns, compared, at least, with the Indy cars, the Winston Cup machines don't come close to matching the speeds of their smaller, distant cousins. In 1996, Arie Luyendyk ran nearly 237 mph to win the Indy 500 pole. The Winston Cup qualifying speeds hover in the 181-182 mph range.

However, because the corners are so square, "It's deceiving how fast you can drive into them," Gordon says. The instinct is to jam on the brakes, but the driver who best feathers the brakes and corners smoothly will be the one winning.

It is NASCAR's dirty little secret that its largest crowds annually watch one of the most boring races because Indy barely is a two-groove track, passing is at a minimum and fuel mileage is frequently a partner in determining the winner.

Indianapolis nearly is fully encircled by stands, from midway on the back stretch all the way around, counterclockwise, to the apex of Turn 2. At the exit of Turn 2 are VIP suites.

More hospitality areas are among the cluster of buildings in the infield adjacent to the front stretch. A 160-foot high pagoda was built in 2000 to serve as media center, control tower and VIP area. The press area is roomy and functional; for the ink-stained wretches of the press, the move to this building from the cramped, antiquated old media room was akin to going from a double-wide to the Taj Mahal. Other suites, leased by various sponsors, are underneath the infield stands.

Gasoline Alley, the garage area, provides roomy, enclosed stalls for all of the entrants. It is guarded by the ever-vigilant band of "yellow shirts," the corps of no-nonsense Indy security guards so named for their unmistakable and bright shirts.

As if Indianapolis Motor Speedway needed another unique touch, it also is the only track in NASCAR that has part of a golf course in the infield. Brickyard Crossing, redesigned into a championship-caliber course in 1991 by the famed golf course architect Pete Dye, has four of its holes in

These are ticket stubs from the inaugural Winston Cup race at Indy, the Brickyard 400 in 1994, as well as the Indianapolis 500 from 1958, 1962 and 1970. The previous year's winner is pictured on the 500 tickets.

the infield. No. 7 is a par 3 over a tiny pond, with the tee box just inside the exit of Turn 2. No. 8, driving to the north, the same direction as cars race on the back stretch, is a par 4 with water all along the left side. No. 9 is a narrow par 4 and No. 10 a slight dog-leg left par 4.

Golf is but a diversion, however. The business of Indy is racing. And business has boomed. The Indianapolis 500, for which TV ratings and overall interest began to wane in the 1990s, was joined here by NASCAR, and finally in 2000 by the SAP U.S. Grand Prix, the first Formula One racing in the States since 1991. A road course was constructed, encompassing Turns 1 and 2, much of the front stretch and a 10-turn road course in the infield.

On August 6, 1994—despite fears to the contrary—the scoring tower didn't collapse into dust. The bricks didn't turn to paste. The sonorous tones of P.A. announcer Tom Carnegie, as integral a part of the speedway as anything, didn't suddenly turn into a Michael Jackson falsetto. The sun didn't refuse to rise.

Winston Cup racing came to Indianapolis.

For the traditionalists, the IndyCar purists, it was sacrilege. The big, heavy-breathing, hulking pieces of Detroit metal didn't belong on this hallowed ground. There was so much talk about "good ol' boys" coming to town, you'd have thought it was a sequel to the Clampetts moving next door to the Drysdale mansion in Beverly Hills.

Since 1911, with the exception of a lone event in September 1916,

Lewis Strang, who started from the pole in the first Indianapolis 500, examines a proposed model of the track. Four identical turns were carved into the dirt.

Indy hosted no race other than the Indianapolis 500. This was as shocking as if Augusta National opened itself for a Putt-Putt tournament. Or if Fenway Park piled in 20 tons of dirt and held a motocross.

Much criticism was heaped upon speedway president Tony George, the grandson of Anton "Tony" Hulman, Jr., the man who rescued the speedway from near-oblivion in 1945 and made it a successful family operation.

But you know what happened?

One tradition was begun without smearing the other tradition.

TRACK FACTS

Size: 2.5-mile oval.
Front and back straights: 3,300 feet.
Short chutes: 660 feet.
Banking: 9 degrees on straightaways, 12 degrees on turns.

Jimmy Spencer on Indianapolis: "I love this racetrack. To me, this is a track where you can't get too aggressive, but you've got to drive on the edge. I love driving on the edge. That doesn't scare me."

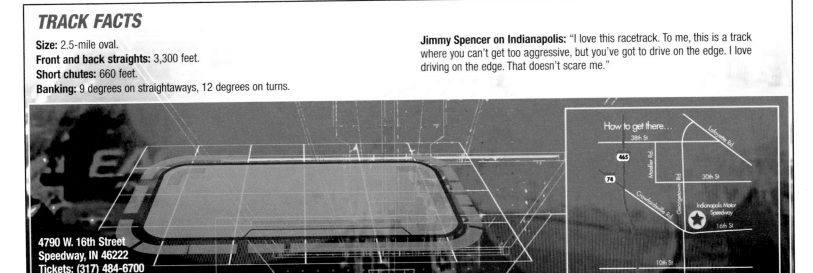

4790 W. 16th Street
Speedway, IN 46222
Tickets: (317) 484-6700
www.brickyard.com

How to get there...

Detente was successful. No family feud after all. The Hulman-George brood on the Indy side could work smoothly with the France empire of NASCAR. The Winston Cup folks, drivers especially, did all the proper P.R. stuff, paying homage to Indianapolis Motor Speedway and treating it as respectfully, as if suddenly invited to spend the night in the Lincoln Bedroom at the White House. So reverent was Michael Waltrip, he didn't even walk out of Gasoline Alley to look at the track before he took his first test lap. "I wanted to be behind the wheel the first time I saw it," he says.

Much as NASCAR is a monster of marketing, it turns out that Indianapolis is, too, down to the deepest roots of its history. When it was built in 1909, it was a test track for the fledgling auto industry. The manufacturers began racing against each other there, in hopes that fans would be lured to buy the successful brands. It may have been much later before somebody in racing coined that old saw, "Win on Sunday, sell on Monday," but the philosophy is nearly a century old. The track surface of crushed rock was too rough on those cars, so track owners brought in 3.2 million bricks—hence the enduring nickname—to build a new surface in time for the inaugural Indianapolis 500, on May 30, 1911. By 1936, asphalt was being applied to some of the rougher spots, and in 1961, the last of the bricks—except for the ceremonial yard-wide strip—was covered.

The first man across the bricks on the last lap of the first Brickyard 400 had spent many an hour at the speedway already.

Jeff Gordon was a Californian by birth but transplanted to Indiana by his stepfather to take advantage of his preternatural racing talent. The first race Gordon attended at Indianapolis, it was in the heyday of the old beer commercial with the "less filling," "tastes great" debate.

"Minutes before the race starts, and the crowd is just starting to get into it," Gordon recalls. "One side is going, 'Tastes great!' The other side goes, 'Less filling!' Just to hear that roar, that was really cool."

His first lap around Indianapolis Motor Speedway was, naturally, in the tour bus. But his prominence as a young driver led to an invite to take his new Chevrolet truck around the track as a teenager.

"It was pretty cool because I was so young, and two, because nobody I knew got to do that."

Gordon was in only his second season in Winston Cup racing when the Brickyard 400 made its debut. It was a homecoming opportunity. It was his birthday. When Ernie Irvan cut a right-front tire late in the race after he had dominated much of the day, Gordon had his chance. He hustled off to victory lane, only his second Winston Cup victory.

"I don't think I'll ever have one that was more memorable or more special than the inaugural affair," Gordon says. "That's just mind-boggling for me to think about it. It was

Stan Fox survived a spectacular crash on the first lap of the 500 in 1995 but didn't drive again. Each winner's likeness is embossed on the Borg-Warner Trophy (left).

The new pagoda, which serves as the control tower, media center and VIP area, was built in 2000. The old pagoda (inset), used for timing and scoring, was torn down in 1986.

only my second year in Winston Cup, and I remember the build-up for that race. What a big deal it was to go to Indianapolis in a stock car. That's just stuff that nobody ever thought would happen.

"I remember how the teams were talking, the buzz. The drivers were like, 'Man, this is a big, big deal, and whoever wins this first one, it would be something.'

"And I wound up winning it."

Lowe's
Motor Speedway

Inaugural race:
World 600, June 19, 1960

The first man who won a 600-mile NASCAR race wore khaki pants and a T-shirt, soaked in a creosote solution to fire-proof them. It took him nearly six hours to finish the race. He was four laps ahead of his nearest competition. His Chevrolet had no power steering.

All of which makes it even more astounding to gaze now upon Lowe's Motor Speedway—or Charlotte Motor Speedway to the traditionalists who keep forgetting (or ignoring) the corporate title purchased in 1999.

Fans packed the grandstands in 1960 at Charlotte Motor Speedway to see the World 600, the track's first race that was won by Joe Lee Johnson in a Chevrolet.

Think of its unique, breathtaking qualities. A fancy lighting system. The largest sporting arena in the Southeast. Two-hundred thousand or so turning out for a race. Condos overlooking the track. A country-club atmosphere in certain exclusive corners.

It's nigh on impossible to take a forkful of prime rib or sip a smooth merlot while sitting in The Speedway Club, seven stories up, and not have your mind boggled by history. It's an astounding Wright Brothers-to-Apollo 11 sort of progression.

But wait. Even that is too much past-tense.

Lowe's Motor Speedway is more like the future of motorsports venues. In fact, it has been the future of motorsports venues since the early 1980s.

Daytona still is home to Winston Cup's preeminent event. Indianapolis, its gates now open to NASCAR, is some racing combination of the Smithsonian Institute and The Vatican. Bristol has more exciting races. A handful of others look newer and boast more novel flourishes.

Still, this place stands apart for so many reasons.

First and foremost, Charlotte, N.C., is the epicenter of Winston Cup racing. Virtually every team, driver and crewman makes his home in the area. High-tech, state-of-the-art race shops are scattered all over, from Mooresville to Concord to Welcome. Drivers are encamped in massive homes along the shores of Lake Norman, north of the city.

Thus, to some extent, Lowe's is everyone's home track, resting as it does 12 miles north of downtown Charlotte, in Concord. It provides, for three weeks out of the season, that most treasured of luxuries, the chance for everyone to wake up in his own bed and go to work, instead of being jarred awake by a hotel alarm clock.

Second, Lowe's has been a pioneer, or at least perfector, of so much. It was the first superspeedway to install a lighting system. It still has the only 600-mile race. It erected condos in 1984. And though VIP hospitality in opulent surroundings has long been emphasized throughout the sport, few places do it better than here.

The infield at racetracks always has been a popular spot for fans, but notice the big difference at 1960 at Charlotte: No motor homes, just cars and a few trucks.

Third, this speedway's success has been the foundation of Speedway Motorsports Inc., which also owns and operates Atlanta, Bristol, Texas and Las Vegas, among other tracks. Bruton Smith, one of the original owners and developers of Charlotte Motor Speedway along with driver Curtis Turner, is the chairman of SMI.

After a slow start in the 1960s, Smith severed his ties, and the speedway fell into bankruptcy. It was rescued by Carolina furniture magnate Richard Howard, who, said Stock Car Racing magazine, "lifted CMS from rocks to riches." However, after an ugly power struggle in the mid-1970s, Smith regained control of the speedway.

Since then, SMI has grown into a powerful entity that enjoys a sometimes fractious, symbiotic relationship with NASCAR but alternately has been a threat, pain-in-the-neck, boon and proud partner for the sport's top panjandrums in Daytona.

If there is a signature spot at Lowe's Motor Speedway, it is the "Humpy Bump." So named in honor of H.A."Humpy" Wheeler, the impresario who serves as the speedway's president and general manager. Wheeler annually bumps up the enthusiasm with prerace extravaganzas in the infield, most of which have been full of two things that strike dear in the heart of NASCAR loyalists: (1) patriotic fervor and (2) blowing stuff up.

The "Humpy Bump" is a spot at the exit of Turn 4 on this 1.5-mile trioval. Hit it wrong, or unsuspectingly, and it has the feel of a catapult, sending the car toward the outside wall.

It is hardly the only obstacle at Lowe's. The turns are banked

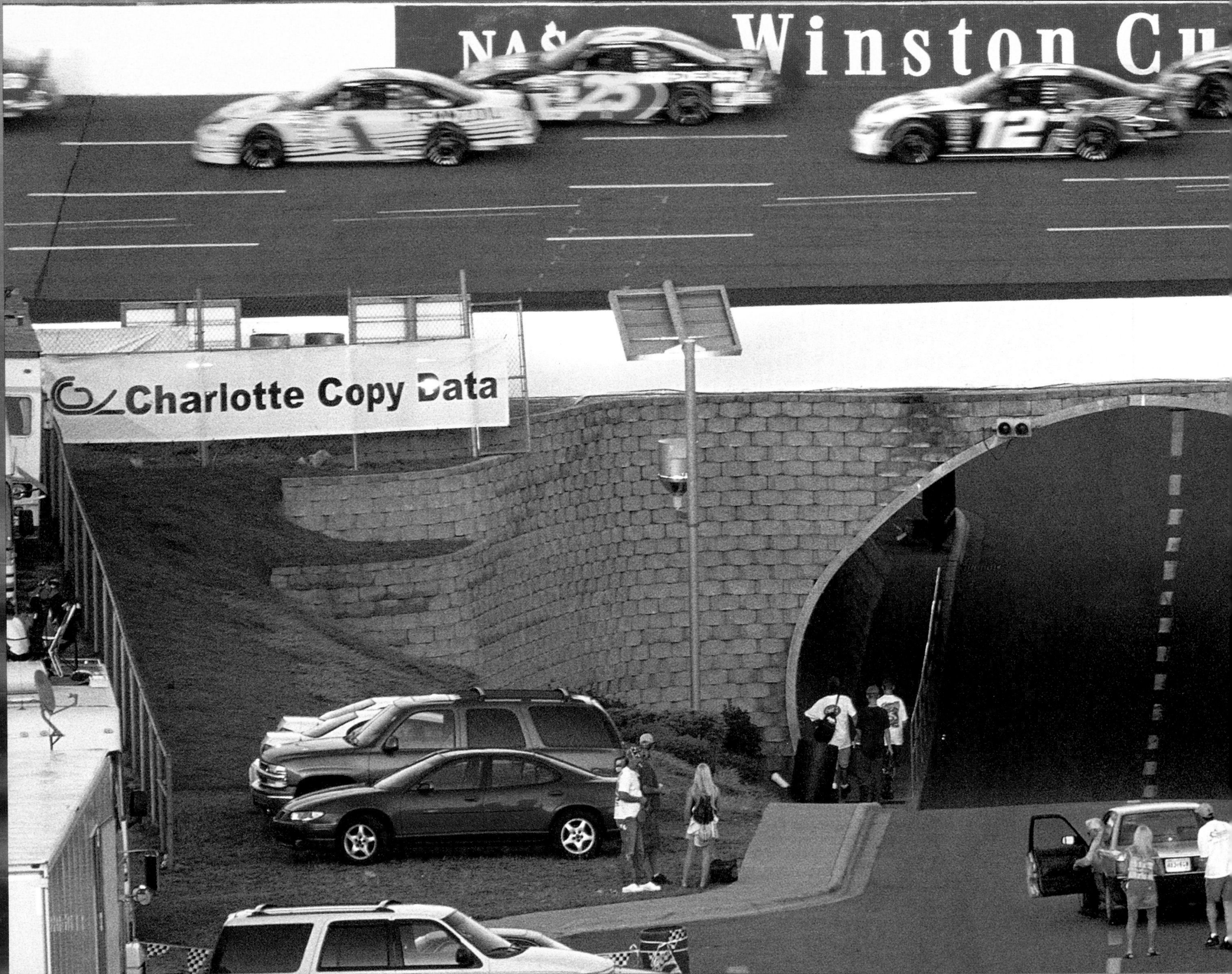
Winston
Charlotte Copy Data

The tunnel that leads into the infield provides entrance and escape for fans and anyone else who wants or needs to beat the traffic even while the cars continue to circle the 1.5-mile track.

at 24 degrees—same as Atlanta—and though the front stretch is nearly 2,000 feet long, it has two treacherous bends along the way. Essentially, drivers are making turns nearly two-thirds of each lap. The relatively long back stretch permits some compelling drag races along the way.

Pity the poor NASCAR chassis specialists who come here. The suspensions must be durable for the long haul of racing. Bad enough there is the "Humpy Bump," and other rough areas. This track evolves into an even more complicated monster because of night-time racing, or day-into-night racing. The track grows fickle and changes as the sun disappears and the temperature falls. A NASCAR crew chief must be prepared to call more audibles than an NFL quarterback once the green flag drops.

The night racing began in 1992, with the installation of a $1.7 million lighting system. Rather than the traditional floodlights seen at most stadiums, it is based on reflective lighting. It has enormous barrel-sized cylinders with mirrors placed alongside the inner ring of the track, with lights beaming into the mirrors. That helps eliminate glare and shadows. It also clicked a light bulb on above the heads of various marketers: Reflective numerals, logos and paint were designed for the cars, which creates a dazzling light show as they loop around Lowe's.

Their parade is performed in front of packed grandstands—Lowe's had more than 167,000 seats by 2002 after a decade's expansion—including the glamourously named "Diamond Tower" on the back stretch. A nice way to sell tickets in an area that, at other tracks, still goes by the unflattering monicker of "Chicken Bone Alley," for the dining choice of its patrons. Turn 4, over the "Humpy Bump," also is prime seating, both outdoors and in the executive suites and box seats. The condos loom over Turn 1.

Along the front is Smith Tower, a seven-story building that

houses the speedway offices, the gift shop and exclusive Speedway Club, with its lunch and dinner seating for 200.

Additionally, Lowe's Motor Speedway has a 2.25-mile road course and a six-tenths of a mile track in the infield, a quarter-mile asphalt oval that encorporates part of the front stretch and pit road and a one-fifth mile oval just outside Turn 3 on the back stretch. In May of 2000, a $9 million dirt track facility was opened across Highway 29 from the speedway.

Several race teams and racing-related industries are on Lowe's Speedway property or adjacent to it. They include a pair of driving schools for mortals who have a little Walter Mitty in their souls. Warning to the fantasy-school racers: Watch out leaving Turn 4. Don't forget the "Humpy Bump."

Six hours away and decades removed, Joe Lee Johnson sat in a small, paneled office above a small racetrack, its clay surface red as blood. It is Cleveland (Tenn.) Speedway, in the Smokies foothills, 25 miles northeast of Chattanooga.

On the wall was a photo of Johnson, standing in victory lane at Charlotte. It was taken June 19, 1960, when he won NASCAR's first 600-mile race—his only victory in what then was called the Grand National series. He wore workboots, a leather helmet, white T-shirt and khakis as his driver's uniform. Though the creosote solution in which he soaked the khakis and shirt might have been a good safety measure, it almost was counterproductive. "They'd rub you so raw and burn you like you were on fire," Johnson said. Just imagine: a six-hour drive, in early summer heat, wearing stiff cotton pants.

Johnson drove a car owned by Paul McDuffie of Atlanta. "Those were truly stock cars. No power steering, and we had those little tires," Johnson said, as if still sore from wrestling

TRACK FACTS

Size: 1.5-mile trioval.
Front straight: 1,952 feet.
Back straight: 1,360 feet.
Banking: 24 degrees in the corners, 5 degrees on the straights.

Bobby Labonte on Lowe's Motor Speedway: "Charlotte is a rough track, so you have to have a good-handling car. Horsepower isn't nearly as important at Charlotte as it is on some mile-and-a-half tracks. If you have a great-handling car, you can win."

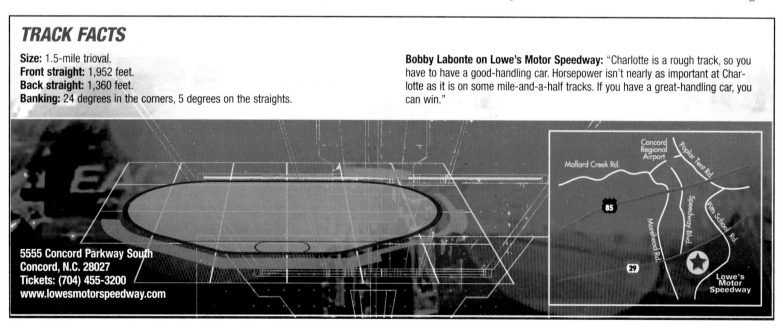

5555 Concord Parkway South
Concord, N.C. 28027
Tickets: (704) 455-3200
www.lowesmotorspeedway.com

the wheel. He was in 20th place at one point but stormed back. Johnny Beauchamp, the runner-up, finished four laps back. Bobby Johns, in third place, was six laps in arrears. Johnson averaged 107.752 mph.

Years later, after McDuffie's death, the winning car was sold at an estate sale. Johnson now regrets not buying it. "If I'd known what I did was going to turn out to be so special, I'd like to have kept the car," Johnson said.

Only a few months earlier, a few miles away, another driver enjoyed his first NASCAR victory. It wouldn't be his last.

The headline in *The National Speed Sport News* proclaimed: "Charlotte GN to Dick Petty"

That's how unfamiliar anyone was with Richard Petty, Lee Petty's young-'un, who had gained only modest prominence with a convertible race victory and another race he lost under protest.

This first of 200 Petty triumphs came at the Charlotte Fairgrounds, a dirt track in the Pineville section. The city was long a hotbed of racing—there are reports of 50,000 watching a race on a wooden track in 1924—and was making its first baby steps toward being the hub of the sport.

The Fairgrounds also was the site of the first NASCAR race in the "Strictly Stock" division that was the forerunner of Winston Cup racing. The inaugural race was June 19, 1949. Jim Roper, in a '49 Lincoln, was declared the winner. That came only after the initial winner, Glen Dunnaway, was disqualified. It seems his team had fudged on the rules and installed illegal rear springs.

So, maybe NASCAR hasn't come that far after all. Indeed, it seems like the more things change, the more they stay the same.

Charlotte, with its condos and suites above Turn 1, was the model for many of the circuit's newer tracks.

Martinsvil
Speedway

Inaugural race:
September 25, 1949

I t is old as your grandfather's pocket watch. And somehow, it's still ticking. Which might be an appropriate analogy because the winner of Martinsville races not only is presented with a trophy that resembles a gargantuan paper clip—it's the shape of the speedway—but also a grandfather clock. Richard Petty won 15 races at Martinsville. Eventually, Lynda Petty, his wife, had to extract all the pendulums from the clocks. The ticking and clanging all over the Petty house got to be too

much of a nuisance.

Martinsville Speedway is NASCAR's oldest—and smallest—track. It is a sepia-colored family portrait come to life. It is almost a homey, country cottage, replete with beds of azaleas and other exquisite landscaping—if you can imagine 43 racecars and a like number of massive tractor-trailers jammed into the driveway.

The speedway is a bridge that spans several eras of transportation. A railroad line, where freight trains chug past at regular intervals, stretches parallel to the backstretch. Nearby, behind the Turn 2 stands, a helipad awaits the frequent arrivals of

It seems there always have been more spectators than seats at Martinsville, even for this 1967 race when a dog strayed in the infield to get a closer look at the action.

corporate big-wigs and drivers who whirl into Martinsville in their ultramodern choppers.

And inside the track, the modern engineering marvels that are Winston Cup cars are nearly as far removed from the pioneer cars at Martinsville as a Model T is from a Learjet.

They travel a distinctive speedway that is flat and skinny, a gridiron of concrete patches. It is a pair of 800-foot straights, connected at each end by what are little more than the sort of tight U-turns you make around a fast-food joint to get to the drive-thru window.

Though Martinsville is barely longer than a half-mile—.526 miles

to be precise—its straightaways are 150 feet longer than Bristol's. So, for two brief moments each lap, drivers pounce on the throttle and hold a little drag race. However, there is but 12 degrees of banking in these tight turns, compared with the sweeping high banks at Bristol that promote high speeds all the way around. The drag races at Martinsville end abruptly.

Martinsville is an incessant cha-cha of "accelerate, brake," "accelerate, brake," "accelerate, brake." No oval track is more demanding on the chassis and brakes than this place. Especially the latter. When TV began to implement its invasive, lipstick-sized cameras all over the cars, someone ingeniously decided to attach one underneath a car and aimed it at the brakes. That demonstrated how rapidly the brakes, glowing as brightly as Rudolph's nose, heated up when a car goes into a corner.

Martinsville hosted its first NASCAR-sanctioned race in 1948, on the Fourth of July. The following season, Bill France Sr. introduced "Strictly Stock," which evolved into the Winston Cup series. Martinsville was the sixth race of that series, on September 25, 1949.

Atlanta, Daytona, Charlotte and Richmond—all of which continue to host NASCAR events—also were on the schedule, but the races were not held in the current locations.

The other races that season were at Danville, Va.; Jacksonville,

The azaleas just above the turns provide a colorful backdrop for the spring race.

Fla.; Macon, Ga.; Augusta, Ga.; Columbus, Ga.; Greensboro, N.C.; Lexington, N.C.; Wadesboro, N.C.; Elkin, N.C.; Occoneechee, N.C.; North Wilkesboro, N.C.; Birmingham, Ala.; Langhorne, Pa.; and Dover, N.J.

All gone by the wayside.

All but Martinsville, which endures in the face of daunting odds.

It endures, as much as anything, because of the legacy of W. Clay Earles, the patriarch of the track who came upon the rolling field next to the railroad line and determined it to be ideal for his speedway.

It was Earles, who died November 16, 1999, at age 86, who insisted the track be so well-manicured with flowers and shrubbery. It was Earles who established a "fans-first" priority. It was Earles who maintained such a long relationship with NASCAR and

the France family, helping ensure Martinsville would not go the way of Langhorne, Pa., and Macon, Ga.

Fittingly for a track that awards grandfather clocks to winners, Earles was grandfather to W. Clay Campbell, who was named track president in 1988.

As NASCAR approached the new millenium, certainly Martinsville's past seemed brighter than its future. Being a small track with limited access and planted in the middle of an already saturated racing marketplace led to the demise of North Wilkesboro, a couple of hours distant from Martinsville. Many wondered how long this track could survive or maintain two races a year.

There was enough sniping at Martinsville from other tracks lusting for a second date that Campbell issued a statement in early 2002. It not only served as rebuttal but as testimony—albeit preju-

The tight quarters in the turns often lead to multicar wrecks because drivers try to outdive one another to gain position. This wreck in the April race in 2000 collected Kyle Petty (45), Kevin Harvick (29), Ken Schrader (36) and Michael Waltrip (15).

diced—to this speedway's charm.

"Some people were quoted ... saying Martinsville shouldn't be on the NASCAR Winston Cup Series schedule. That irritates not only me, but all the fans who have supported this track since I was just a boy. Martinsville helped make NASCAR what it is today.

"Our track has grown and made many improvements over the years. It just irritates the heck out of me when I hear some other track operator talking about big markets and all that other self-serving stuff. It's my understanding our races draw higher ratings than a lot of the other tracks do. The biggest problem fans have here is not knowing which way to look. There is action everywhere, every lap. There's something going on all the time."

Martinsville indeed has done its best to keep pace and to accomodate as many fans as possible since Campbell took over in 1988. It nearly is surrounded by seating areas. The capacity was doubled. Some 25 VIP suites were added. The Blue Ridge Tower looms 66 rows high over the start-finish line. Other stands stretch high, like gigantic fans, in Turns 1 and 2. But Campbell and Co. remained true to Earles' legacy in one sense. There is a "Family Section" on the back stretch, between the racetrack and the train tracks, where unreserved seats go on sale on race day only. Children's tickets are absurdly inexpensive, especially in the NASCAR marketplace. They come with one rule: Adults must be accompanied by a child for admittance into the area.

More than 42,000 seats were added here in a building boom of the 1990s—while North Wilkesboro, its neighbor to the south, was unable and unwilling to expand—as well as more parking and amenities. To the delight of race teams, a new garage area and a

Size: 0.526-mile oval.
Front straight: 800 feet.
Back straight: 800 feet.
Banking: 12 degrees in the corners.

John Andretti on Martinsville: "You don't have to do that old deal of slamming into their rear end, get them half sideways and go underneath them anymore."

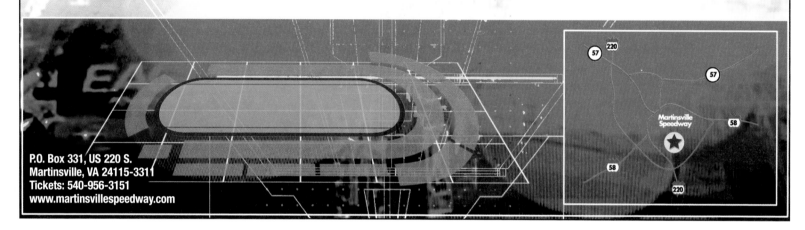

P.O. Box 331, US 220 S.
Martinsville, VA 24115-3311
Tickets: 540-956-3151
www.martinsvillespeedway.com

tunnel into the infield were added in 2001, helping ease the terrible congestion in the limited area of the Martinsville infield.

Perhaps, for too many years, Martinsville had been aligned more closely to North Wilkesboro as a dinosaur in a small town, destined to become extinct in the modern NASCAR world. Instead, Martinsville was more akin to Bristol, ever-expanding to permit as many fans as possible to see old-style, bullring, close-quarter racing.

By Earles' count, there were 6,013 fans watching—with seats for only 750—on September 7, 1947, when the narrow dirt oval opened 2 miles south of Martinsville, nestled in

the foothills of the Blue Ridge Mountains between Roanoke, Va., and Greensboro, N.C. Red Byron won the 50-lap feature and pocketed $500.

The next year brought the first Martinsville race sanctioned by NASCAR, but 1949 stands as the year that NASCAR, as we know it, was created. Byron, in an Olds 88, won that race.

Here is how it was covered in *The Martinsville Bulletin*:

"Clyde Minter Is Fourth In Stock Car Race," read the headline above a three-inch story.

"Clyde Minter of Martinsville, driving a Ford car in his first

automobile race, finished fourth yesterday at the local speedway.

"Red Byron, who was the winner of the first race at the Martinsville track two years ago, was the winner again yesterday.
His time for the 200 laps was one hour and 57 minutes.

"Fonty Flock was in the lead when he blew out a tire on the
90th lap. In this grueling race, all of the drivers encountered
trouble. Curtis Turner of Roanoke broke a spindle on his Olds on
the 50th lap.

"With only a few laps to go, Byron lost a wheel, but he had a
big lead and was able to win handily after having the wheel
replaced.

"A large crowd was on hand to witness the first race here
strictly for stock cars.

"Lee Petty of Greensboro was second, Ray Erickson of Chicago
third."

The Martinsville dirt oval was paved over and made asphalt in
time for the 1956 race, won by Buck Baker, then, in 1976, Earles
ordered some concrete patches placed on the track where the
asphalt had grown flimsy. All it did initially was promote controversy in the racing fraternity. Then, as speeds increased and
track durability was proved, once again it proved Earles to be a
wizard.

Concrete and azaleas and concrete. Satisfied customers.
Thrilling racing. Earles' legacy continues, tick-tick-ticking away
into a new millennium.

The closeness in distance
of the crews gathered for the national
anthem shows that pit road
here is tight, too.

North Caro
Speedway

Also known as:
Rockingham; The Rock

Inaugural race:
American 500, October 31, 1965

Not far away from North Carolina Speedway—better known as Rockingham, or simply "The Rock"—is the golf mecca of Pinehurst. It is a picturesque little village of boutiques and bed-and-breakfasts, surrounded by plush courses. Pinehurst No. 2, the site of the 1999 U.S. Open, is the most famous and challenging of them all.

"The man who doesn't feel emotionally stirred when he golfs at Pinehurst beneath those clear blue

Cars roar down the front stretch during one of the first NASCAR events at the track, which opened in 1965.

skies and with the pine fragrance in his nostrils is one who should be ruled out of golf for life," wrote the golf legend Tommy Armour. "It's the kind of course that gets into the blood of an old trooper."

Perhaps that's a tad too eloquent for racing. And the bit about pine fragrance should be replaced by the sweetly acrid smell of Union 76 racing fuel.

But, you know, Rockingham does get in your blood.

"I really like the racetrack," said Ryan Newman before a Rockingham race. "It's a lot of fun. It's a driver's racetrack."

It's a testy ol' rascal, a broad oval that has different banking at each end and relatively wide straightaways (50 feet). Both are true straightaways, without the bulges of the modern-day triovals. The banking around Turns 1 and 2 is at 22 degrees. It grows steeper on the other end, at 25 degrees, in a long, sweeping curve of 1,400-plus feet—longer even than either straightaway—

Scoreboards and billboards have come a long way since 1965, but even then advertisers were pushing their products to fans. The scoreboard reveals that No. 43, Richard Petty, started from the pole in the track's first race, the American 500.

and plenty wide for two grooves of racing. Rockingham is, as they say, just a tad off plumb. It is 17/100 (or 90 feet) longer than a mile, leading to the bit of arithmetic that decides a 400-mile race in 393 laps.

It has a rough surface that gnaws at tires like a cheese grater on a wedge of cheddar. It is the same sort of abrasive track as Darlington, seemingly full of sand both in composition and simply collecting on the surface, and tire wear frequently becomes the determining factor here.

"Throughout the race the track becomes really greasy, causing cars to lose grip and start slipping and sliding all over the place," Ricky Rudd has said. "While cars begin the race at the bottom of the track, by the end, they're right up there against the wall. There is 'elbow room.' But you have to find which groove your car runs the best on to move forward."

There is almost an old-style football stadium feel to

the seating. The Rockingham Grandstand, crowned by 34 VIP suites, runs along the front. The Hamlet Grandstand rises above the back. However, there is seating for little more than 60,000. Therein lies a problem for this scuffed-up antique. Its seating capacity is the smallest on the Winston Cup circuit. For years, there was speculation it soon would become extinct, like North Wilkesboro. The speedway now is property of the International Speedway Corporation, NASCAR's sister organization. ISC had acquired Penske Motorsports in 1999, two years after Roger Penske bought the track from the DeWitt family.

Geography works both in The Rock's favor and future, and against it. It is in the "Sandhills" area of North Carolina, in the southern part of the state, 10 miles from the town of Rockingham, 20 miles south of golf-crazy Pinehurst. More broadly, it is just 75 miles from Charlotte to the east, 90 miles from Raleigh to the north. For fans' convenience, Amtrak even initiated the "Rockingham Race Special," nonstop service from Raleigh with a variety of packages that even include race tickets and an Amtrak hospitality pass.

However, for some, The Rock is considered too close to home. There are eight races a year within two hours of Char-

Kenny Wallace, who was subbing for Steve Park in the yellow Pennzoil car, works lapped traffic in the 2001 Pop Secret 400.

lotte, counting Martinsville, Darlington, Charlotte and Rockingham. For a sport that is searching for every opportunity to stretch its boundaries and reach larger metropolitan areas, that's too many in one area, stretching the fan and marketing dollars way too thin.

Rockingham also must share that support base with its next-door neighbor, Rockingham Dragway, just down Highway 1 from the main entrance to the speedway. The quarter-mile asphalt strip hosts opening and closing annual events of the IHRA schedule as well as another three-dozen events.

Rockingham is a track of firsts.

Around NASCAR, there is the broad sentiment that "it's really the first race of the year." It comes on the heels of Daytona, which is such an extended, distracting spectacle for drivers and teams. Though the Daytona 500 is the season's most famous and lucrative event, there is a sense that it's not pure racing, what with the cars choked by restrictor plates, swept away in aerodynamic quirks and unable to pass effectively.

Dale Jarrett doesn't go quite that far, but he has said, "There is so much work and effort that go into preparing for Speedweeks and the Daytona 500 that it makes Rockingham a very welcome event. The season starts with the dropping of the green flag in

North Carolina Speedway faces many challenges, including just 60,000 seats.

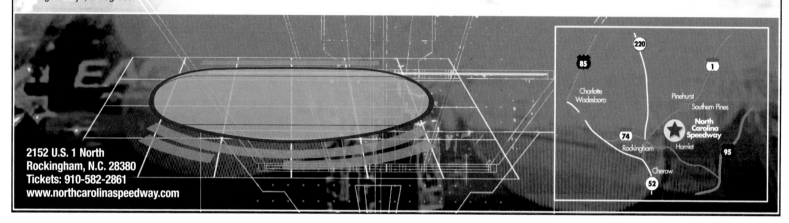

TRACK FACTS

Size: 1.017-mile oval.
Front straight: 1,300 feet.
Back straight: 1,367 feet.
Banking: Turns 1 and 2, 22 degrees; Turns 3 and 4, 25 degrees; front and back straightaways, 8 degrees.

Joe Nemechek on The Rock: "Rockingham eats up tires like Godzilla eats those little Japanese soldiers in the movies. The teams that deal with it the best are the ones you are going to find up front by the end of the day."

2152 U.S. 1 North
Rockingham, N.C. 28380
Tickets: 910-582-2861
www.northcarolinaspeedway.com

the 500, but Rockingham is where we actually dig in to the schedule and get started on the routine we'll have during the next 10 months of the year."

It was the site of Johnny Benson's first Winston Cup win, in October 2002. The next morning, his children Katelyn and Mikayla, asked if they could take the trophy to school for "show and tell." Sorry, kids. Daddy had a TV show to tape. He had his own "show and tell." The trophy went to the studio.

It was the site of Mark Martin's first Winston Cup win, in October 1989. It was the site of Jeff Gordon's first substantial laps inside a stock car. Gordon, the open-wheel prodigy from Indiana, came south to Buck Baker's driving school at Rockingham to become acclimated to the bigger racecars.

It was the site of the first Winston Cup races for an 18-year-old

Rudd and Bill Elliott—in a powder-blue Ford Torino, with which he won a whopping $640—among others.

It was the site where NASCAR had to shrug off its mourning period and go back to work, the first race after Dale Earnhardt's death in 2001.

It was a pivotal site for Darrell Waltrip's first Winston Cup title, stretching a win streak to four races—his bitter rival in those days, Bobby Allison, was runner-up in three of those—with a triumph in the American 500, the springboard to the 1981 championship.

It was the site of a seismic return to the sport by Curtis Turner, the old Virginian who drove nearly as hard as he partied. Turner had tried to organize a drivers' union in the 1960s, under the umbrella of the Teamsters, and a livid Bill France Sr. banished him from the sport. He allowed Turner back in 1965, in time for the American 500 at Rockingham.

It was, in fact, the speedway's first race. Driving a Ford owned by Glen Wood, and suffering from a broken rib, Turner outlasted young Cale Yarborough for the win. They were the only two on the lead lap.

The track was a project of landowner Bill Land and Harold Brasington, who earlier had put his signature on NASCAR with the development of Darlington Raceway. It was flat, one-mile track in those days, nothing like Brasington's curious egg-shaped, banked oval at Darlington.

L.G. DeWitt, a local trucking company executive, ultimately took over The Rock, and during his 20-year reign as president, the original flat track was transformed into the banked 1.017-mile oval in 1969. That was the first time a computer was used to design a track.

An annual highlight since 1967 has been the Union 76 World Pit Crew Competition, held the Saturday before the fall race here. It is the only NASCAR-sanctioned pit crew contest on the circuit.

Each crew in the top 25 in Winston cup points is eligible. Cars screech on to pit road and are filled with two seven-gallon cans of gas, and all four tires are changed as fast as possible before the car is sent back out. Penalties are assessed, adding precious seconds to scores, for mistakes such as loose lug nuts, spilled fuel, etc.

The Rock's improvements in the 1990s made it a much better place for those crew members to work. Enclosed garages were built in 1996, replacing the open-air stalls that left teams so vulnerable to the angry, icy late February chill that tends to attack this place. A new pit road assured that each team would pit on the front, eliminating the disadvantage for the lower qualifiers who had been sentenced to the backside pit road.

An annual highlight at the track since 1967 has been the Union 76 World Pit Crew Competition, held the Saturday before the fall race. For a long time, crew members didn't wear protective gear.

For all the changes, there has been one constant. Out in front of the track is a symbol to the track's toughness, a large granite rock adjacent to the speedway offices. One of NASCAR's most hoary traditions is that the winners at The Rock have their names engraved on the rock. There is plenty of room on the rock for more.

Richmond
International Raceway

Inaugural race:
Richmond 200, April 19, 1953

Cruise slowly down Monument Avenue, the broad, tree-lined boulevard with its eclectic architecture and grassy median. Along the way are towering, distinguished links to the past, the statues of various Confederate heroes. Few cities are more awash in history than Richmond; few cities embrace and cherish that history as much. This is one of the city's most famous and well-traveled streets.

Almost incongrously among the Civil War generals, Monu-

ment Avenue's final statue is a tribute one of Richmond's greatest sons, the tennis player and humanitarian Arthur Ashe. The bronze statue shows Ashe with books in one arm, a tennis racket in the other.

Monument Avenue is symbolic of the marriage of past and progress that is so much of this grand city's charms.

Five miles away, in another little corner of history, past and progress also is symbolized on a D-shaped bit of asphalt.

Richmond International Raceway rests in the same spot where its first automobile race was held in 1946, where the city's first NASCAR event was held in 1953. Yet any similarity to the past is mere coincidence. Progress brought a dramatic, stunning face-lift.

Lee Petty won the first NASCAR race here, driving a Dodge. Richard Petty won a record 13 races here, including seven in a row. Mostly, he was driving a Plymouth. When Kyle Petty became the first third-generation racer to win a Winston Cup race, it was here in 1986 in a Ford.

But more symbolism here—the most important Petty vehicle, from a Richmond perspective, was the bulldozer onto which King Richard clambered on the evening of February 21, 1988, in post-race festivities. He ceremoniously cranked up the bulldozer and

Crew members attend to a car during a 1971 race at Richmond. Richard Petty's two victories there that season began a streak of seven consecutive wins at the track.

dug up some turf to begin an ambitious construction project that turned an uninspiring, mediocre racetrack into a speedway that epitomizes the best NASCAR has to offer.

Slow to convert to modern-day racing, Richmond stubbornly remained a dirt track until 1968. Once paved, it was a nondescript half-mile. Then, with the impetus of the broadly respected and admired track owner, Paul Sawyer, Richmond did more than catch up to the rest of the racing world. It began to surpass much of it.

Richmond International Raceway is Winston Cup's only three-quarter mile track, with comfortable banking, wide racing area and seating for nearly 100,000. And every seat is treasured. Racing here at night is a spectacular show. Lights gleam off the reflective paint of the cars. Flames belch from exhaust pipes, and sparks fly when metal brushes metal or cars bottom out on the pavement, offering the sort of fireworks typically reserved for July 4.

The closest parallel to Richmond is Bristol Motor Speedway, a quarter-mile shorter. Like Bristol, Richmond proves you can cram in 100,000 or so souls around a smaller track, hold a dramatic race with high-wire tension for the fans and please the drivers. Not every new track, the lesson at Richmond says, has to be the same mile-and-a-half blueprint. The next new speedway developer who steals Richmond's design will be proclaimed the next new innovative, gutsy genius in this sport.

Witness this conversation between a media member and Rusty Wallace:

"What's the perfect racetrack?"

"Richmond," Wallace quickly answered.

"So," Wallace was asked, "if you were in the racetrack business and you could build a new track today, what would you build?"

"I'd build another Richmond," Wallace said. "It's just the perfect size. It offers super competition ... great side-by-side racing ... and there's plenty of room for everybody. They could keep adding seats at that place if they wanted to. I think everybody loves Richmond."

Richmond has long, broad straightaways, with two distinct grooves that are conducive to passing. There is much side-by-side racing, sometimes going on lap after lap. The front stretch ends with a little bump before entering Turn 1, which can throw off the entrance into Turn 2. But most drivers point to the exit of Turn 4, to take advantage of a 1,290-foot straightaway, as the key, especially because that straight often leads to close-quarter racing.

Oldtimers still get chill-bumps thinking of old Dale Earnhardt-Wallace waltzes, going door to door as if no other cars were on the track. It's still quite physical, almost encouraging some good-natured paint-swapping. But it's a little more forgiving than those "self-cleaning" banks at Bristol, where one bobble can lead to a junkyard. So physical, some of NASCAR's great feuds have been ignited—or settled—here.

All of which seems to have great appeal to fans, who gather in stands that wind completely around the track. There typically is a waiting list for tickets. Traffic often is horrendous. An enterprising aviation company offers its services—for a premium price—to the

Cars head toward Turn 1 in the 1999 Pontiac Excitement 400 that was won by Dale Jarrett.

Dale Earnhardt Jr., in his final full season in the Busch Series, gets tires and fuel during a 1998 race at Richmond. He won and finished second in two races there that year.

track via helicopter, landing just outside Turn 2.

What's the old Yogi Berra line? The place is so crowded, nobody goes there anymore. Same here at Richmond. "The traffic is a joke. I won't go again until I can afford the helicopter ride," said one Richmond resident.

Complicating the traffic is the speedway's location. Richmond International Raceway and Indianapolis Motor Speedway are the only tracks on the Winston Cup circuit located in the middle of major cities. Other tracks near large metropolitan areas are located at least on the fringe of development or well out of the city center. Richmond is sandwiched among neighborhoods and businesses along Laburnum Avenue, offering a challenge for the traffic gurus in Henrico County.

The track is the heart of the Richmond Raceway Complex,

Rusty Wallace, who considers Richmond the perfect racetrack, sits on the pole at the start of this race—the 1991 Miller Genuine Draft 400.

the relatively new title for the sprawling property. It still might be better known as the Virginia State Fairgrounds. Or even its past mouthful moniker, the Atlantic Rural Exhibiton Fairgrounds. Or Strawberry Hill.

It is surrounded by the typical accoutrements of a fair—an amphitheater, stockyard buildings, flea-market booths, the vast open spaces where a carnival almost can magically appear overnight with a midway full of lights, noise and joy.

Richmond's fair officials and others of influence have sought to move the fair elsewhere from these grounds, and certainly one less livestock arena would be much needed parking for the race. Sadly for some, one casualty of the speedway growth was another bit of horsepower. The "Strawberry Hill Races," a festive steeplechase equestrian event that had been a tradition since the late 1800s, also was held at the fairgrounds from 1949 until 1999, when the International Speedway Corporation purchased Richmond International Raceway.

That sale—for a reported $215 million—was the most expensive, but not necessarily most monumental, transaction and transition in Richmond's saga.

Like so many of its brethren in the post World War II era, Richmond's speedway was a rugged dirt track, a fickle place for cars, a difficult place for drivers and uncomfortable to even the most hardy fans battling the eye-watering dust. The first race was held here in October 1946, but the first official NASCAR Grand National event didn't take place at Richmond until April 19, 1953, with Lee Petty winning.

Two years later, Paul Sawyer and driver Joe Weatherly purchased the speedway, and it continued to thrive as a regular stop on the NASCAR circuit and a venue for local racers. Eventually, Sawyer recognized the need for progress and ordered the dirt surface to be paved, and it was re-measured at .625 miles in length. Despite the asphalt, old photos still show massive clouds of dirt as cars dive onto the apron of the track on a tight turn, with rows of pine trees forming the backdrop behind the planked fencing that served as the outer barrier.

It was all well and good for another two decades. Though the occasional tweaking changed the length, shrinking gradually with each improvement, Richmond became too unwieldy simply to take a Band-Aid approach to repairs and changes.

Sawyer went to the fairgrounds board and, according to *Stock Car Racing* magazine, said, "Gentlemen, I can't patch this one any more. Can I tear it down and rebuild?"

When he received the affirmative answer, Sawyer got busy. In a hurry. He called upon Charles Moneypenny, the architect who also designed Daytona and Michigan's speedways, to create the revamped facility in Richmond.

The late Neil Bonnett, an easy-going Alabama driver, won the final race on the old configuration, in February 1988. After that race, Petty mounted the bulldozer to symbolically begin the renovation.

The next September 11, almost poetically, the first race at "new" Richmond was won by Davey Allison, Bonnett's friend and protege.

Sawyer later recalled the changes, saying, "I called it the 10th wonder of the world because everyone said we couldn't do it."

In 1991, he added more wonder—a lighting system. "I was looking at the romantic end of it, too," Sawyer said. "It's a completely different atmosphere from a boiling-down hot Sunday afternoon to a nice, soft Saturday night. And it reminds people of back in the old days at Columbia and Hickory—the hundred-milers they ran at night."

More progress. And a substantial nod to the past.

TRACK FACTS

Size: .750-mile oval.
Front straight: 1,290 feet.
Back straight: 860 feet.
Banking: Turns 14 degrees; front straight, 8 degrees; back straight, 2 degrees.

Rusty Wallace on Richmond: "It's just the perfect size. it offers perfect competition, great side-by-side racing, and there's plenty of room for everybody. They could keep adding seats at this place if they wanted to."

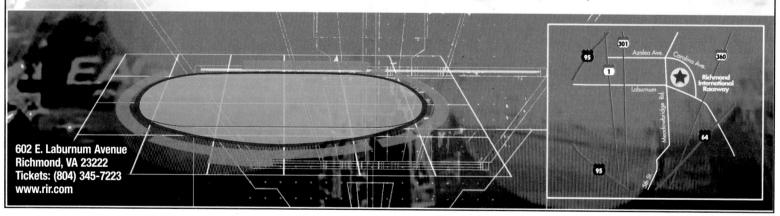

602 E. Laburnum Avenue
Richmond, VA 23222
Tickets: (804) 345-7223
www.rir.com

Fans watch the early laps of the 1998 Exide Batteries 400 as the last bit of sun disappears on the horizon behind Turns 3 and 4.

Modern

Dover

International Speedway

Nickname:
The Monster Mile

Inaugural race:
Mason Dixon 300, July 6, 1969

"The Monster Mile?" How about a "Monstrous Multiplex?" Or "Monstrous Millions-Maker?"

Who could have imagined that a humble little harness-racing track in a picturesque little city would have evolved into this booming, unique creation? Who could have foreseen how this essential Southern sport would have bloomed in this gateway to the Northeast?

Dover International

Speedway—the Dover Downs tag was dropped in 2002—is the monster that NASCAR drivers attempt to slay twice yearly. It is a mile-long oval of concrete, an unforgiving layout with steep banks that promote high speeds and often unavoidable crashes. It is a test of endurance and patience, as much as a test of skill and automobile. As little children sleep fitfully with visions of monsters under their beds, "The Monster Mile" causes more than a little tossing and turning and nightmares among racers.

But this is no longer a mere racetrack, no more than one can call Disney World a place with a few rides. With vision, benevolent politics, good fortune and, as real estate agents would put it, location, location, location, Dover has become one of the most incredible and fascinating growth stories in the racing business.

Let's take Dover as if a fruit and peel back the layers.

First, on the outside, standing sentry over the back stretch, is the Dover Downs Hotel and Convention Center. It has 10 stories, 240 rooms and suites, six restaurants and bars and the largest ballroom in the state of Delaware. Half of the rooms overlook the speedway. The retail promenade from the hotel leads to

The proximity of the racetrack to Dover Air Force Base has created a symbiotic relationship with NASCAR.

an 80,000-square foot casino with 2,000 slot machines. The casino is connected to the air-conditioned grandstands on the back stretch of Dover, overlooking the speedway.

Finally, running alongside the concrete track for race cars is the gray ribbon of the five-eighths mile harness track, where racing takes place November through April. It is part of a newly created gaming-industry con-glomerate noun: "racino." It has made Dover unique as a NASCAR venue, and made the owners a fortune. In 1994, the state of Delaware passed a law permitting video casinos at horse tracks. Cha-ching! That was like pulling triple cherries on the slot machine. Lights went off, sirens wailed and coins clanged in a joyous cacophony. Within four years, revenue leapt from $1 million to $81 million, according to reports. Dover Downs Gaming & Entertainment Inc., became publicly traded in 1996.

Dover Motorsports, Inc., was spun from that. It built the spiffy new track outside Nashville, and operates tracks in Memphis and St. Louis. It promotes several Grand Prix events. But the roots, and the greatest success, is still the Monster.

The winningest drivers at Dover have been guys such as Brad

Hanners, Eddie Davis and Luc Ouellette. They are among the chariot drivers at Dover Downs' harness track that opened in the early 1960s. Ouellette, if this helps, can be considered the Jeff Gordon of his sport. Ouellette wins something like 11 out of every 100 races.

More significant horsepower arrived in 1969, with another "winningest driver" commanding attention. Richard Petty, NASCAR's all-time wins leader, collected Nos. 96 and 116 on his way to 200 victories by capturing the inaugural Mason-Dixon 300 on July 6, 1969—collecting a hefty $4,725 in finishing six laps ahead of his nearest pursuers, Sonny Hutchins and James Hylton —and repeating in 1970. In 2002, a NASCAR rookie, Jimmie Johnson, joined Petty in the history books. He pulled the

"Dover Double," becoming, along with Petty, the only driver to win back-to-back in his first two appearances at a track.

In its early days, Dover was a tire-grinding asphalt track. It was an unfriendly surface because of the sealer track officials used to patch the winter-battered asphalt. Finally, in 1995, the concrete surface, less affected by weather, was installed. That provided one of those "good news, bad news" situations. Good news, in that more racing grooves were available—though woe be to a driver who strays too high and into the loose "marbles" of tire residue. Bad news in that, as Gordon put it once after a win here, "There's no easy way around Dover."

With its steep, 24-degree banking, it is a perilous track. Racers have limited vision for trouble looming ahead, and with the high

The Monster Mile is the primary attraction when NASCAR visits twice each year, but the facility has grown into the most unique on the circuit in that it also is home to a harness track, hotel and convention center and an 80,000-square foot casino with 2,000 slot machines.

speeds Dover yields, chain-reaction accidents are often unavoidable. There is almost never a single-car wreck here. Because the banking is steep, drivers refer to Dover as "self-cleaning." Gravity takes over quickly after the carnage, with cars sliding toward the infield rapidly. Knowing that, drivers try to avoid accidents by veering high, along the wall, but sometimes that causes a sudden bottleneck as bad or worse than the collision.

It was appropriate that Dover, in 2001, honored one of the region's most famous athletes. Cal Ripken Jr., the Baltimore Orioles' legend, was retiring. The fall race was named the MBNA Cal Ripken Jr. 400. It was a fitting honor because Ripken achieved his greatest renown by establishing the longest playing streak in major league baseball, earning an "Iron Man" status in the minds of sports fans.

Dover required "Iron Man" endurance from drivers for years. The races from 1971 to 1997 were a seemingly interminable 500 miles in length. "The 24 Hours of Dover," some called the races here. The monotony of the 500 one-mile laps, the inevitable many cautions that delayed races and tendency of some drivers to run off and leave the field led to long, boring afternoons. For the benefit of weary drivers and crews, to ease the long day for fans and, mostly, to condense the event into more palatable television viewing, both Dover races were shortened to 400 miles by 1998.

Even so, this is not a speedway the majority of drivers happily anticipate visiting. And that's not the way to deal with a monster. "If you dread it or just don't feel good about it or whatever, you don't stand a chance," Kyle Petty has said. "The place is tough, really tough. The races can be pretty hard. You have to be in great shape. But you'd better walk in there thinking, 'Man, I really love this place. I can run well here.' Or it's

TRACK FACTS

Size: 1-mile oval.
Front straight: 1,076 feet.
Back straight: 1,076 feet.
Banking: Turns, 24 degrees;
front and back straights, 9 degrees.

Tony Stewart on Dover: "You just try to keep up with the track conditions. Nothing else really changes. But that doesn't mean you can get lazy. If you just assume that you're going to be good, that's when you're going to get beat because guys are going to make changes."

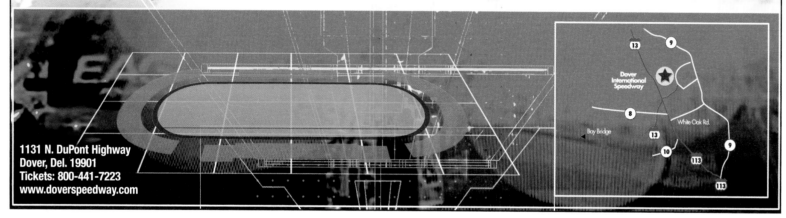

1131 N. DuPont Highway
Dover, Del. 19901
Tickets: 800-441-7223
www.doverspeedway.com

going to be a long weekend."

Dover was an important venue for NASCAR as it began to stretch beyond its Southern roots in the late 1960s. NASCAR already was making regular visits to California. In 1969, Dover joined Michigan and the late, lamented Texas World Speedway on the NASCAR schedule. Dover might have been the most symbolic stop as the Southern sport reached out to Northern audiences. After all, the Mason-Dixon line—the namesake of the inaugural race—runs nearby. Delaware was a divided state in the Civil War.

In the 1970s, the speedway could legitimately bill itself as having drawn the largest crowds for any sporting venue between Yankee Stadium and Charlotte. Even still, fans pour from up and down the Eastern Seaboard. Amtrak introduced a "Dover Downs Express" train, running from New York City to the speedway on

race weekends. It is a critical spot for NASCAR's business, with four of the top eight media markets within an easy trip to Dover.

It's certainly critical to Dover's business as well. It is a lovely city, rich with history. Its downtown boasts "The Green," a lush area encircled by renovated 18th Century buildings, and "Legislative Mall," where the state capitol, designed in 1717, resides.

Turning from the past, almost futuristic creatures reside south of town. Dover Air Force Base has created an almost symbiotic relationship with NASCAR. Many of the Winston Cup teams land there for the Dover race. Graphic artists have incorporated a checkered flag into a Dover AFB logo. The Air Force has had associate sponsorship on a number of cars. Seldom does a Dover race weekend take place that some Winston Cup driver isn't getting red-carpet treatment at the base, all under the watchful eye of some TV network cameras.

Dover AFB is home to the 436th Airlift Wing, and more C-5 Galaxy transport planes than anywhere. The C-5, with its large-mouth bass front end and 222-foot wingspan and 247-foot length, is the largest airplane in the free world. It can hold six busses in its cargo hold or, in a rare bit of Air Force P.R. whimsy, it is "large enough to haul ... 25,844,746 ping-pong balls."

If there were ever doubts of NASCAR's popularity in these parts, they were dispelled decades ago not only with the monstrous crowds at The Monster Mile, but even later in the day, as dark falls over Delaware. Fans established a neat tradition. The NASCAR team haulers would leave Dover on narrow two-lane highways, headed across the Delmarva Peninsula into Maryland, to hook up with I-95 South and the route home. Fans lined the highway on both sides, watching the convoy of haulers stream past. Fans waved homemade signs and sported the souvenir garb of various drivers. Amazing. More than 100,000 to watch cars race ... and still hundreds more simply to watch the handsome transporters.

No word on how many ping-pong balls might fit inside one of those haulers.

Steep banking and limited sight for drivers are reasons multicar wrecks occur in the turns at Dover.

Michigan

International Speedway

Inaugural race:
Motor State 500, June 15, 1969

A h, if only every road leading into the place was as wide and cozy and forgiving as Michigan International Speedway itself.

The Irish Hills, into which Michigan International Speedway is nestled, are lovely and lush. Immigrants from the British Isles to this part of the state in the late 19th century noted the similarity in terrain, climate and vegetation to the rolling hills of Ireland. Hence the name.

The 50 or so lakes in the area are placid mirrors onto which rolling forests of green are reflected. Quaint little towns pop up every now and then to interrupt miles of farmland. It is an area of bed-and-breakfasts and small diners, instead of chain motels and familiar fast-food joints. It is a land of antique stores, with their special gee-gaws and gimcracks spilling onto porches, and farm-equipment supply houses with gleaming tractors standing guard outside. Marinas and quaint cottages and luxury vacation homes encircle the lakes.

There is a severe consequence of such pristine, natural beauty:

Winding, crowded, antiquated two-lane highways.

Going to a race at Michigan frequently can be a long day's nightmare of traffic. Small-town stoplights prompt bottlenecks. Small-town gendarmes aim their radar guns at unsuspecting visitors. A pokey motor home or a tractor that strays from the fields, taking the highway back to the barn, will dissolve a race-goer's patience.

But escape the highways, pull into one of the grassy parking lots or the massive infield, and it's wide-open spaces—on and off the track.

Michigan International Speedway is a 2-mile, D-shaped oval. It is broad and long, banked just perfectly enough. The turns are 73 feet wide and banked at 18 degrees.

As a result, there are three adequate racing grooves. To see cars

Michigan is one of many tracks that host NASCAR and open-wheel races. Mario Andretti watches son Michael exit the pits in 1998.

going four-wide in places is not unusual, nor especially alarming. At most tracks, three-wide invites trouble. Two solid and equal racing grooves are a luxury. Not so at Michigan. It becomes as much a matter of driver preference and reacting to the car's particular handling characteristics on that day or at that moment when choosing a path to follow around Michigan.

The speedway pooches out slightly on the frontstretch, like a man's middle-aged bulge, and the back stretch is straight. Because a little more speed is generated there, it makes Turns 3 and 4 a little more treacherous, especially on a hot afternoon as the track gets more slippery. But for the most part, Michigan is a smooth, comfortable ride where the drivers must feather the throttle just so on entrance to the turns, without letting up too much.

Says Michael Waltrip, "It seems like momentum is the most important thing."

Because it sits only 90 miles west of Detroit—albeit a difficult 90 miles—Michigan is an important stop on the circuit. Its fans are especially brand-loyal and knowledgeable, this close to the capital of the American automotive world. Many of the patrons are intimately connected to the auto industry.

That proximity to Detroit convinced Roger Penske to make the speedway a beautiful, first-class site when he assumed receivership of the track for $2 million in 1973. It needed not only to be a magnificent speedway but also a hospitality venue. Come race weekend, Michigan becomes a schmooze-a-rama. There are more deep-pocketed sponsors and VIPs at Michigan than anywhere except Daytona, Charlotte, and now, perhaps, for reasons other than geographical convenience, Las Vegas. Michigan also needed to be a versatile speedway that could host the open-wheel cars from Indianapolis.

Penske had 26 pit road terrace suites constructed on the inside of the track, aware of how much the pit road hubhub seemed to delight the moneyed folk who hung out in hospitality suites near

Gasoline Alley at Indianapolis. The terrace suite patrons have a bird's-eye view of the frenetic action on pit road as well as the racing on the 3,600-foot front stretch. Penske multiplied his initial investment countless times over, adding 100,000 grandstand seats, numerous buildings and other accommodations before merging his publicly-traded company with International Speedway Corporation, Daytona's parent company, in 1999.

Part of the investment also was a greater amount of safety measures. In 1998, in the U.S. 500 Indy Racing League event, Adrian Fernandez hit the wall between Turns 3 and 4, one of his tires

Mark Martin says there is "just enough banking" at Michigan to run fast, whether it's stock cars or open-wheel racers.

and many pieces of debris launched into the grandstands. Three spectators were killed.

Michigan's partnership with Daytona completed the picture with much symmetry. Michigan had been designed by Charles Moneypenny, who also designed Daytona International Speedway. Moneypenny had been commissioned by Michigan's original owner, a Detroit developer named Lawrence H. LoPatin, who built the speedway for, according to various reports, anywhere from $4 million to $6 million.

The consequence of such generous racing surface: Less-than-scintillating races.

Michigan's size and design have made it one of the "cleaner" tracks on the circuit. It doesn't have the configuration or length to put such an overwhelming emphasis on drafting, so bumper-to-bumper-to-bumper racing, like the 20-car trains at Daytona and Talladega, is not as frequent. The width of the track provides more room and is more forgiving of slight bobbles or momentary loss of control that might lead to accidents elsewhere. With so many equally efficient grooves, it never seems crowded.

Because there are so few wrecks, there often are few cautions. That means that gas mileage often becomes a deciding factor, and the field becomes more strung out. Michigan also seemed to be dominated by individuals on hot streaks, who seemed to have the place figured out better than anyone else.

Bill Elliott won four in a row here in the 1980s, and six out of nine. David Pearson won seven of nine in the 1970s. Mark Martin won four races here in the 1990s, appropriate because this is virtually the back yard for his car owner, Jack Roush.

The dominant car owners, though, were the Wood Brothers, with 11 wins between 1969 and 1991.

TRACK FACTS

Size: 2.0-mile, D-shaped oval.
Front Straight: 3,600 feet.
Back Straight: 2,242 feet.
Banking: 18 degrees in corners, 12 degrees on frontstretch, 5 degrees backstretch.

Mark Martin on driving at Michigan: "It's a real racetrack where the fastest car wins. There's just enough banking, and you can run any groove—low, middle or high—and the track is wide enough that there's plenty of room to pass the slower cars. I like going to Michigan because we always have a good shot to win."

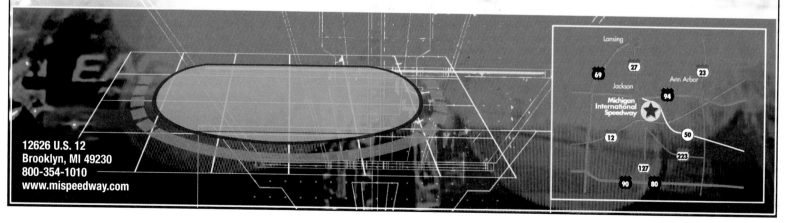

12626 U.S. 12
Brooklyn, MI 49230
800-354-1010
www.mispeedway.com

It's organized chaos on pit road during this stop in 2002. Pit stops are an important part of every race, but fuel strategy often comes into play at Michigan because there are few cautions.

That began with the inaugural race, the Motor State 500 on June 15, 1969. Cale Yarborough and LeeRoy Yarbrough were separated most of the day by even less than the extra "o" in Cale's last name. On the first turn of the last lap, after they had been beating and banging on each other on the straightaway, LeeRoy slapped the wall. He regained momentum and re-entered the chase, only to spin out 300 yards from the finish line as Cale won in a Wood Brothers Mercury.

Even more dramatic, Dale Jarrett won his first NASCAR Winston Cup race there in August, 1991, edging Davey Allison by a matter of eight to 10 inches. Allison was driving for Robert Yates Racing,

for which Jarrett won the 1999 Winston Cup championship. Jarrett was in the No. 21 Citgo Ford of the Wood Brothers. Allison had dominated much of the afternoon. Then, with 12 laps remaining, a caution came out. Jarrett and the Woods opted to pit for gas only, and Allison and Yates went for fresh tires. Jarrett came out of the pits in the lead, but Allison soon was able to catch up. Jarrett maintained the preferable inside position, but Allison's fresh tires helped him stick right alongside Jarrett, the two cars sharing the same shadow. Like Yarborough and Yarbrough 22 years earlier, they clanged on each other's fenders and doors all around the track. Jarrett, at the proper moments, managed to make his car "wider," gobbling up enough speedway with defensive blocking maneuvers, to keep Allison at bay until the final sprint off the final turn. One more lap, maybe even 20 more feet, and the outcome might have been different.

Fate and Michigan treated Allison and his family even more cruelly. In 1992, his brother Clifford was killed during practice for a Busch Series race.

In August, 1994, driving for the same Havoline Texaco No. 28 Thunderbird team for which Davey Allison once drove, Ernie Irvan slammed violently into the wall during a practice session. Initially, doctors gave Irvan only a 10 percent chance of survival. Even after Irvan's miraculous recovery, they warned him he'd be lucky ever to drive on the highway again, so severe was his head injury.

Irvan was a gutsy, aggressive driver, always a factor in the early 1990s. At times he was a bit reckless. After one near-disastrous move of his caused a major crash, he went hat-in-hand before his peers at a drivers' meeting before a race, acknowledging his mistake and vowing to be a smarter, more patient driver.

Dale Earnhardt Jr. greets Muhammad Ali before the June 2001 race at Michigan.

The man who once earned the criticism of his fellow competitors earned their unanimous admiration after the near-fatal wreck at Michigan. He made a courageous comeback in 1996, winning a pair of races. Then, on June 15, 1997, there was Ernie Irvan, in victory lane at Michigan. "It was a case like I had conquered the racetrack that almost conquered me," he said.

In the harshest of irony, Irvan later collided with Michigan's wall again, sustaining a head injury that led him to announce his retirement in September 1999.

"First of all," Irvan said later, "that was (the site of) my last Winston Cup win, so it's special in my heart. Then you look at it and it's like, 'OK, that's where both wrecks happened, so you must not like Michigan.'

"But when it's all said and done, the people at Michigan International Speedway are the ones who saved my life. I owe a lot to the racetrack and all the people they had put in place."

New Hamp

International Speedway

Nickname:
The Magic Mile

Inaugural race:
Slick 50 300, July 11, 1993

Breakneck speed. Bumper-to-bumper-to-bumper dueling. Maniacal, aggressive drivers all jockeying for the same precious spot of real estate. Out-of-control turns at terrifying speed. Endless circles of traffic. Chewed up roadways, with booby traps of potholes, and marbles of asphalt rattling in share-drum sounds on the car's undercarriage.

That's driving in New England.

But ... enough about

Boston drivers, roadways and traffic.

Let's go 80 miles north, to the lovely piney woods in central New Hampshire, where perhaps the kinship among drivers and spectators has made tickets to the two yearly Winston Cup events precious commodities.

It is New Hampshire International Speedway, aka "The Magic Mile." Indeed, it has been a magical NASCAR success story on one end of the spectrum. At the other end, it has been a miserable mile, rife with controversy and tragedy.

New Hampshire was the first domino to topple over, beginning the dizzying boom of speedway construction in the 1990s. For 20 years, no one was bold enough to build a new major speedway. NASCAR was a regional sport, saturating the southeastern United States, then making the occasional foray north and west to whet the appetite of the growing legion of fans elsewhere.

Enter Bob Bahre.

He already was one of the sport's most beloved figures, an avuncular, self-made man who rose from childhood poverty to become a millionaire developer and real estate tycoon. He was a racedriver and race promoter. More than that, a race fan. His brother, Dick, had owned or co-owned several Winston Cup teams.

With no guarantee of landing a Winston Cup event, Bahre constructed this 1.058-mile speedway, using $30 million of his money. He created a dream. And, too often, a nightmare.

In 1988, Bahre purchased Bryar Motorsports Park in Loudon, 10 miles or so from the state capital of Concord. It was a popular spot for the sports-car set since Keith and Rose Bryar opened it in 1965. It featured a pond alongside the course from which the occasional driver and car had to be fished.

Bahre demolished the park but only after assuring a road-course circuit would be built at New Hampshire International. He filled in the lake. To abide by the strict conservationist laws of the state to preserve waterways, he had to build another lake nearby. No problem. He needed the fill-dirt anyway.

New Hampshire International Speedway debuted in 1993 with a monumental buzz. The New England fans poured into the place. The New England media gobbled it up. *The Boston Globe* devoted its entire Sunday front sports page to racing on the inaugural Sunday. It was pretty and pristine and, until the motors roared, downright peaceful in this remote locale on a two-lane highway well off the interstate. Rusty Wallace won that race, on July 13, 1993, despite starting 33rd.

Since that day, this speedway also has hosted the open-wheelers from the IRL and CART, motorcycle and go-kart races and, true to Bahre's word, sports-car events on its road course.

The track, in design, is somewhere between, say, Dover and Phoenix. It has long straightaways and short turns but only slightly banked—at 12 degrees. The banking is just steep enough to maintain speed but flat enough to require a delicate approach and caution. It is symmetrical, like Dover, but with 1,500-foot straightaways, longer than tracks of similar length like Dover and Rockingham, and only a smidgen shorter than the Phoenix back stretch.

Grandstands stretch their arms to snuggle the whole front stretch, from the bend entering Turn 4 all the way around to the apex between Turns 1 and 2.

Truth is, it still wasn't enough seating, but Bahre was smart enough to (1) make tickets seem like a premium and (2) realize that he had enough traffic and parking woes without adding to them. As it was, fans were being ferried from distant lots by school buses or from distant spots in the parking lots by trams.

New Englanders have been quite taken by this place, the largest

sporting arena in the Northeast. Including one Maine native named Ricky Craven, a NASCAR veteran who all but gushed about it in a 2000 nascar.com interview.

"How I view New Hampshire International Speedway, as an athlete, is the same way I grew up, as a New England boy with Fenway Park," Craven said. "New Hampshire International Speedway, to me, is what the Boston Garden is to basketball or what Fenway Park and the Green Monster are to a baseball player. New Hampshire is New England's track."

Alas, some of Craven's peers have been less charitable with their praise.

"Like running on crushed ice."

"A sandbox."

"Worst racetrack I've ever raced on."

"Unacceptable."

Those were some reviews for NHIS as it approached its second decade of racing. No speedway on the Winston Cup circuit copes with such drastic weather as this one does. The frigid winters are followed by summers that grow deceptively scorching; visitors to the inaugural event vividly recall the legs of their camp chairs sinking 2 inches deep into the marshmallowy, fresh asphalt in the garage area.

The track surface has taken a beating because of the weather and some egregious paving mistakes to which constructions companies confessed. Said Jeff Gordon, heading toward a New Hampshire race after still another attempt by the track to repair and

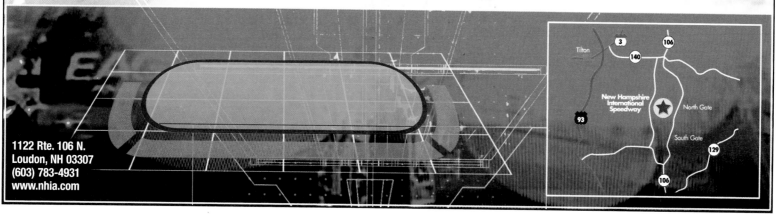

TRACK FACTS

Size: 1,058-mile trioval.
Front straight: 1,500 feet.
Back straight: 1,500 feet.
Banking: 12 degrees in the corners; 5 degrees
on the back stretch, 3 degrees on the front stretch.

Joe Nemechek on New Hampshire: "You've got to drive into the corners as hard
as you can, and the track is trying to make you make a mistake."

1122 Rte. 106 N.
Loudon, NH 03307
(603) 783-4931
www.nhia.com

repave, "I love Bob Bahre. He's my favorite track owner out there. But they've got a real problem up there."

In 2002, Bahre ordered the racing surface widened along the inside, adding more racing room if not exactly another groove on what remains barely more than a one-groove track, and flattened the transition area onto the apron.

A deteriorating track surface hardly has been the worst of the problems.

In 2000, two drivers were killed here. Adam Petty died in a crash during Busch Series practice May 12; Kenny Irwin died July 7 while practicing for the Winston Cup event. Both wrecks occurred in almost the same spot, treacherous Turn 3, into which cars enter at great speeds after the dragstrip of the long back stretch.

By then, New Hampshire had been awarded two Winston Cup races a year. Even that was controversial. Bahre and Bruton Smith

both purchased half-interest of the North Wilkesboro Speedway in 1995. They have yet to agree what should be done with North Wilkesboro. But there was no argument what they would do with North Wilkesboro's two dates on the Winston Cup calendar. Smith took one for his Texas Motor Speedway, and Bahre took the other for a second race at New Hampshire.

That second date, as you might suspect, was the one to which NASCAR was headed on the week of September 11, 2001. It was postponed, naturally, until late November, when racing folks feared that snowmobiles or dogsleds would be more appropriate than Fords and Chevys.

And did we say that all of New England had embraced this speedway? Let's amend that. One of the closest neighbors is "Shaker Village" in Canterbury, a living museum that demonstrates the lifestyle of the Shakers, a religious sect grounded in simple, quiet life. They filed suit against Bahre to prevent an expansion of the track, claiming he and the speedway were guilty of destroying their quality of life.

In even greater irony, Bahre also found himself in court against the owners of Maine's Oxford Plains Speedway. Once, Bahre had owned that very track, a three-eighths mile oval. Back in the 1960s, when the NASCAR circuit seemingly appeared in a different venue every day, like the Harlem Globetrotters or some rock band, Bahre brought three Winston Cup (then Grand National) races to Oxford Plains. Bobby Allison won the first one, then Richard Petty the next two. The Busch Grand National circuit raced there into the 1990s.

Oxford Plains, a few hours away to the northeast, was clearly the predecessor to New Hampshire International Speedway in terms of NASCAR's toehold on New England. But the new owners charged Bahre with "irreparable harm" in their 2000 lawsuit against him.

It all seems way too much tumult for an area so tranquil.

NHIS is at the southern edge of New Hampshire's popular tourist

New Hampshire's racing surface is decried by many as the worst on the circuit. Here, Kyle Petty takes a spin. In 2000, Kyle's youngest son, Adam, was killed in a Turn 3 crash, the same turn in which Kenny Irwin was killed in a crash two months later. Race workers (below) paid tribute to Irwin later that weekend.

region, with quaint bed-and-breakfasts, antique stores and other businesses relying heavily on words like "ye olde" and "shoppe." It is near the Lakes Region, dominated by Lake Winnipesaukee, with its 72 square miles ringed by cottages and resorts. Lake Winnipesaukee is a popular spot for those who wish to incorporate a little serenity and sanity with the madness of a race weekend, especially as the fall race brings a hint of the glorious fall colors that seem to turn the entire state into a palette of reds, golds and oranges.

Above it all looms Mount Washington, with its near-constant scalp of snow. At 6,288 feet, it is the highest peak in the northeastern U.S. Almost perversely, park officials suggest that Mount Washington has "the world's worst climate." Indeed, meteorologists once measured winds of 231 miles per hour on its peak.

An area that weathers that sort of brutal gust and then still emerges as something as grand and gorgeous as New Hampshire autumns ... well, surely that should stand as some metaphor for the future of New Hampshire International Speedway.

Phoenix

International Raceway

Nickname:
The Desert Jewel

Inaugural race:
Checker 500, November 6, 1988

These are the coolest, most spectacular cheap seats in all of sports.

As the races begin at Phoenix International Raceway, a handful of spectators appear high on the craggy hilltop behind the back stretch. They canter up on horseback and watch the race from their saddles. There they sit, framed by azure skies and a couple of cotton-candy clouds and mountaintops and Saguaro cactus, like some scene from an old Western movie. They

are poised as if waiting to gallop away to head off somebody at the pass rather than watching cars trying to pass who's ahead.

While watching the race, they also must watch for some other varmints. Among the most pesky denizens of the desert are rattlesnakes. The track officials, in fact, send some brave specialists out into the parking area and territory around the track on race week to rustle up the snakes. A few of the rattlers even have been discovered snoozing away in the cool shade of the garage area.

It's not as if we're talking about a snake pit from an Indiana Jones movie. Herpetologists tell you that rattlers are as afraid of you as you are of them. Highly unlikely, right?

But to bask in this majestic desert setting, with its typically impeccable weather, it's worth stepping lightly.

Such are the immediate environs of Phoenix International Raceway, one wouldn't be surprised to see Wile E. Coyote screaming past on roller skates, with an Acme rocket pack attached to his back, chasing that elusive Road Runner. Appropriate to its desert surroundings, this track virtually is flat. The banking in Turns 1 and 2 is 11 degrees; it's merely 9 degrees in Turns 3 and 4, the same as Indianapolis Motor Speedway.

Each turn is unique, presenting a challenge in setting up the chassis. What works in Turn 1 might be counterproductive in Turn

This cactus serves as a reminder that Phoenix International Raceway was plopped into the desert.

4. The heat—even in November—makes the track slippery. A crew chief who is unable to make adjustments throughout the course of the day is a crew chief destined to leave Arizona with a 20th-place finish or worse.

The track further is complicated by a screwy little dogleg on the back stretch. It looks almost as if the track designer hiccupped when he was sketching the back stretch on his blueprints.

Turns 1 and 2 are all but the same, a hard left almost as tight as Pocono's treacherous first turn. The back stretch, despite the little dogleg, is plenty long to build up speed as the folks on horseback watch from above. It's also a good passing spot, especially by outbraking the competition heading into Turn 3.

The entrance to the infield and garage area is in the mouth of a gate at Turn 2. A road course also snakes through the infield. A crossover bridge—interrupting in-car camera shots with static and a crackly picture—stretches across Turn 4. Though it is a 1-mile track, the Winston Cup races here are measured in kilometers. The 312 laps are equal to 500 kilometers.

The track butts up against the Estrella Mountains and native American lands to the south. Monument Hill, a rocky, virtually barren peak, guards the track over Turn 3. Close by are the Salt and Gila Rivers, both of which are dry beds much of the time.

Each turn of the 1-mile track is unique, which presents a challenge for those who must set up the chassis.

When they become real rivers, watch out. Until a $10 million bridge was built at the last bend heading into the track on 115th Street, floods threatened to maroon folks at the speedway.

The speedway officially is in Avondale, 15 miles west of downtown Phoenix, 5 miles off Interstate 10, which eventually leads to Los Angeles.

When NASCAR first came to Phoenix, this truly was a trip to the desert. Now, it's a visit to suburbia. The small ranches and farms and small touches of industry spread out in grids are evolving into residential neighborhoods, indicative of the constant growth in "The Valley of the Sun."

Despite the growth and limited access roads to the track from Interstate 10, Maricopa County was in 2002 presented an award by the National Association of Counties for success in managing traffic. That could prompt a chuckle. Racing fans know that here, or anywhere else, the phrase "race-day traffic management" is an oxymoron.

Emmett "Buddy" Jobe anticipated the land boom outside Phoenix. He had seen the area grow from a desert town melting all over itself in the summer, with water a precious commodity. By the 1980s, with air conditioning and irrigation, Phoenix and its environs became a business hub, a golf haven and a refuge for retirees.

Jobe saw Phoenix International Raceway as an investment. It wouldn't be for racing cars. It would be for racing other developers to the bank. This would be prime land as Phoenix expanded west. He purchased the property in 1985 from race promoter Dennis Wood solely as a land investment. Jobe paid $2.75 million and proudly told people he wrapped up the deal by signing "a single document on the hood of my pickup."

Says Phoenix motorsports journalist Mark Armijo, "He didn't think he'd be there all that long. But he got hooked. The sport bit him."

It still rains in The Valley of the Sun. But even then, Phoenix has a reputation for being one of the most picturesque settings in the series.

Jobe began to make improvements on the speedway. He built more grandstands—there were fewer than 10,000 seats when he bought the track—parking, amenities, etc. He added a wonderful midway area behind the front-stretch stands. The racing world loved the place. Phoenix always was a popular stop for the NASCAR family despite the distance. Especially in the days when a week off preceded the race, Phoenix was a splendid working vacation trip. For those not tethered to their cars and forced to work every waking moment—in other words, sponsors, owners and media—there could be side trips to the glorious red mountains in Sedona, the Grand Canyon four hours to the north or the cowboy town of Tombstone to the southeast. For those with deep pockets, there was golf and spas and pampering for bigwigs and their families at the many posh resorts.

Ultimately, Phoenix International Raceway became one of the most incredible investment successes in all business, not merely NASCAR. A dozen years later, Jobe sold the track to International Speedway Corporation—which also owns Daytona and Talladega, among other venues—for some $60 million.

Phoenix International had been running open-wheel races for two decades before Jobe came along. A.J. Foyt won the 100-mile Governors Cup USAC event there in 1964, and Lloyd Ruby a 200-miler. USAC, and its successor CART, visited Phoenix twice a year. Hence the racing tradition of naming grandstands for prominent drivers mixes company here. Bobby Allison and Richard Petty grandstands sandwich those named for Foyt and Jimmy Bryan.

Before this track came into existence, Arizona's racing hub was at the Phoenix Fairgrounds, not far from the center of the city. (Unless, of course, one wants to consider a four-car, 500-mile race across the desert from Los Angeles to Phoenix, which the winner completed in a mere 30 hours, 36 minutes.) The mile-long dirt

TRACK FACTS

Size: 1-mile oval.
Front straight: 1,179 feet.
Back straight: 1,551 feet.
Banking: Turns 1 and 2, 11 degrees; Turns 3 and 4, 8 degrees; front and back straights, 0 degrees.

John Andretti on Phoenix: "The track is fast enough that you can cut a lot of laps pretty quick and slow enough that if a guy runs into you, you can sometimes save it instead of bringing out a yellow."

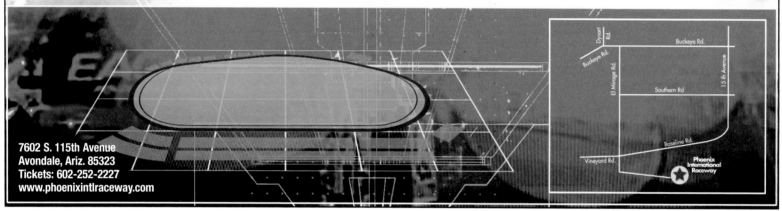

7602 S. 115th Avenue
Avondale, Ariz. 85323
Tickets: 602-252-2227
www.phoenixintlraceway.com

track, which began holding races in the early 1900s, eventually became too dangerous and difficult. Richard and Nancy Hogue, members of the Phoenix sports car set, decided to build a permanent road course track west of Phoenix. USAC pleaded with them to build an oval course, which could include the road course. Hence the relatively flat banking.

NASCAR arrived in 1988 for the Checker 500. It coincided with another arrival of sorts.

A solemn young man with an mechanical engineering degree from the University of Wisconsin had been toiling on the Winston Cup circuit for two years. He owned his own car. He had a stubborn independent streak.

On November 6, 1988, Alan Kulwicki came from 21st place to win his first Winston Cup race, the inaugural Phoenix event. He punctuated the day with a curious move. He did a U-turn on the front

stretch after taking the checkered flag, and began to traverse the track clockwise. A "Polish Victory Lap," he called it. Kulwicki won four more races before his death in April 1993, in a plane crash.

The 1996 winner was a soft-drawling Tennesseean named Bobby Hamilton. It was just dessert in the desert for Hamilton.

Seven years earlier, Hamilton was an unofficial entrant in the Autoworks 500. He was driving a car equipped with cameras. NASCAR had permitted the producers of the movie *Days Of Thunder* a spot in the field so up-close, realistic footage could be filmed. Hamilton would motor along near the rear of the field, out of harm's way.

Trouble was, Hamilton was a racer at heart. And his car was even better than folks figured. In the middle of the race, NASCAR officials had to radio the movie people and Hamilton to have him slow down.

The hill above Turn 4 (inset) provides a unique view for fans while the track sits beneath the Estrella Mountains, not a bad view for drivers.

POCONO
Raceway

Inaugural race:
Purolator 500, August 5, 1974

Any geometry student can reel off names of triangles: acute, isosceles, pocono, equilateral, obtuse, scalene.

OK. So one of them really doesn't belong on that list. But, it turns out, it's the most complex and perplexing triangle of them all.

Pocono Raceway is a 2.5-mile chunk of geometry in the mountains of eastern Pennsylvania near a village called Long Pond.

It rests in a lush, green region, easily accessible to

Drivers—that's Jeff Gordon with his legion of fans—generate a lot of speed on Pocono's straightaways ...

... but they have to get on the brakes and downshift to maneuver through the track's unique corners.

New York City, Philadelphia and other large cities of the Northeast. It long has been a prime vacation spot, dating even to the 19th century, with its lovely mountains and breathtaking scenery. It is best known for its large number of romantic lodges, with their heart-shaped tubs and cozy fireplaces, that cater to honeymooners.

There is nothing lovey-dovey about Pocono Raceway—unless you consider that it requires a harmonic marriage of driver and car. It couples the longest straightaway in Winston Cup racing with three turns that must be approached as gingerly as if walking with slick-soled shoes on a patch of ice.

"I don't think there's a place like it on Earth," Elliott Sadler

says. "It's just three totally different turns, with three totally different bankings. And you have to give up a little here and there to be good in one turn, and you have to give up some in another one."

No matter how much you give, Pocono typically takes more than its should.

Were it a bit wider, you could land a Boeing 767 on the frontstretch. It is 3,704 feet long. You don't so much follow the cars as you watch them materialize, or disappear, over the horizon. By the end of the stretch, they're hitting nearly 200 mph. But only briefly. As Turn 1 looms, drivers are gouging at the brakes, downshifting and preparing to yank things down from full speed

Drviers say Pocono requires road-course skills: nursing their cars through the different corners while maintaining speed for the straightaways.

into a near-hairpin turn. Pocono provides "crib notes" of sorts to help drivers cheat at the end of the front. Along the wall are "countdown" signs, providing points of reference that Turn 1 is approaching quickly.

Though they can go four- and five-wide with ease on the front, drivers begin dicing for the preferred inside line for the track's first elbow, banked at 14 degrees. They let the cars drift toward the wall out of Turn 1. Frequently, drift turns into disaster. Carry too much speed into Turn 1, and the centrifugal force slings cars into the wall.

The "Long Pond" straightaway is next, another 3,000 feet and change. It introduces the sharp, 90-degree "Tunnel Turn," so far removed from the main grandstands that it seems in another area code.

Turn 3 comes at the end of a short chute, the 1,780-foot North Straight. It's essentially a flat, lazy, sweeping turn and is especially slippery in hot weather. Take it slow ... but not too slow. If you ease up too much here, it'll take too long to get up to high speed on the runway, er, front stretch.

Drivers compare Pocono with a less-harmonic marriage—road

course and superspeedway. The speeds can be Talladega-ish. But the tight turns require the gear ratios and chassis set-ups of a road course. Not to mention the incessant shifting and braking required from the driver behind the wheel.

It is not a symmetrical triangle. It's a little lopsided to the left because of the shorter North Straight. No such thing as perfect geometry. But imperfection is part of Pocono's charm.

So, just who is the Dr. Frankenstein who put together these spare parts and made a speedway out of them?

Credit—or blame—Rodger Ward. An old World War II fighter pilot, Ward won a pair of Indianapolis 500s and enjoyed a racing career that earned him induction into the International Motorsports Hall of Fame. He was the Pocono Raceway designer.

Ultimately, though, the credit should go to Dr. Joe Mattioli and his wife, Dr. Rose Mattioli. Dr. Joe purchased a 1,025-acre area of forest land and a spinach farm in the 1960s near the tiny burg of Long Pond, tucked away in the lush, green Poconos. (The mountains' name comes from an Indian word meaning "a stream between mountains.")

At first, it was a meager three-quarter mile track. The Mattiolis

Drivers who visit victory lane at Pocono, like David Pearson did in 1975, know they have tamed a difficult racetrack.

then enlisted Ward to design this current incarnation, and the first 500-mile event was the 1971 Schaefer 500, an Indy-car race. Workers still were painting numbers on grandstand seats the night before the race. NASCAR came a-calling in 1974. Richard Petty won the inaugural event.

But Pocono Raceway, for the Mattiolis, became a stream of money between mountains, flowing away. Several times, the track was on the brink of bankruptcy. The track was one of many innocent victims in the civil wars that seem constantly to plague the open-wheel world of Indy cars. The Mattioli Family was going to sell the track. However, Dr. Joe and Dr. Rose were invited to New York one day to meet Bill France Sr. He encouraged them to stick with it. He promised a pair of races each year would be awarded to Pocono.

As they parted, France handed Dr. Joe one of his business cards. On the back, Big Bill had scribbled a message: "On the plains of hesitation lie the bleached bones of millions who when within the grasp of vistory sat and waited and waiting died."

Soon, things began to blossom at Pocono. It benefited from NASCAR's broad, nationwide appeal and the vast Northeastern population base. Interstate 80, 3 miles from the speedway, was

TRACK FACTS

Size: 2.5-mile trioval.
Front straight: 3,740 feet.
Long pond straight: 3,055 feet.
North straight: 1,780 feet.
Banking: Turns 1: 14 degrees, Turn 2 The Tunnel Turn: 8 degrees, Turn 3: 6 degrees.

Bobby Labonte on Pocono: "It's a tough track. You have to make the proper (handling) adjustments to make the car stick, or you'll be slipping and sliding a lot."

Long Pond Road
Long Pond, PA 318334
(800) RACEWAY (722-3929)
www.poconoraceway.com

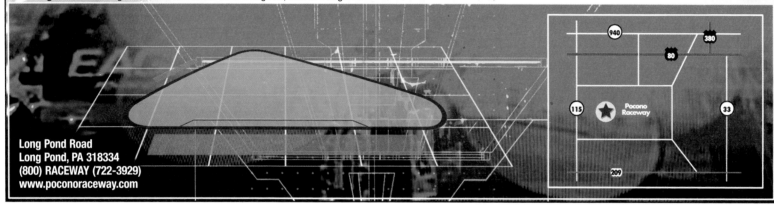

guaranteed to turn into a parking lot two Sundays a summer, when fans rolled in from big cities and tiny towns. To reward the fans, the Mattioli family reinvested millions. They created a Paddock Area in the garage for fans to get up-close looks at the cars and teams. They built a picnic area with gazebos and added 14 40-foot tall spruce trees and 200 picnic tables. They even took care of the drivers, with one of the finer infield motorhome lots on the NASCAR circuit.

Alas, there would be no heart-shaped tubs in the motor-home lot.

Maybe because Pocono is an amalgam of so many different tracks—a dash of road course here, a dab of superspeedway there, a smidgen of Indianapolis thrown in for seasoning—Tim Richmond had the place mastered. In a meteoric career, he proved he could drive anything, anywhere. He was the 1978 Rookie of the Year for USAC sprint cars. He was the 1980 Indy 500

Rookie of the Year. He landed in NASCAR and seemed destined for superstardom.

Richmond won 13 Winston Cup races in 185 starts. Four of those came at Pocono, where he made his NASCAR debut in July 1980, having been invited by Dr. Joe Mattioli, who noticed his skill in the Indy 500.

Richmond was a handsome, flamboyant character, the antithesis of the flinty good ol' boys who still ruled NASCAR in those days. He had long hair and wore fancy suits and flashy jewelry. He was a favorite of female fans. He galloped up to the track on a rumbling Harley-Davidson. Richmond was a free-spirit who never met a party he didn't like.

Yet he mixed perfectly with the curmudgeonly crew chief, Harry Hyde, and the successful Charlotte auto dealer and businessman Rick Hendrick. That relationship was at the core of Hol-

Pocono's front straight is massive—at least four grooves wide and almost long enough to land a jetliner.

lywood's early 1990s treatment of NASCAR in *Days of Thunder*, with the open-wheel refugee, played by Tom Cruise, venturing into NASCAR.

In 1986, Richmond won seven races and eight poles. He was elected as "driver of the year," though Dale Earnhardt won the second of his seven Winston Cup titles.

However, Richmond became, and still is to an extent, NASCAR's little family secret, spoken of only in guarded whispers. Late in 1986, his friends and fellow drivers noticed a change in him. He didn't seem healthy. He missed the 1987 Daytona 500 with what then was reported as double pneumonia. Rumors of drug abuse circulated. NASCAR announced a suspension for violation of the drug policy, only to have to rescind the

suspension when the drug was proved to be an over-the-counter cold medicine. Still, he was sick and withdrawn. He was wrestling with the secret that he had been diagnosed with AIDS in December 1986.

Richmond gained enough strength to get back in a racecar in the spring of 1987. He came here to Pocono in June, and won the race—his third straight triumph at Pocono. He broke down in tears at the finish line and was so emotional he needed a second victory lap to get his composure. Richmond made it back-to-back victories the next week, at Riverside.

He never won another race. And on August 13, 1989, he died in West Palm Beach, Fla. Ten days later, the family finally unlocked the secret, that Richmond died of AIDS.

Talladega

Superspeedway

Inaugural race:
Talladega 500, September 14, 1969

You're on your first lap around Talladega Superspeedway. You have buckled yourself in the passenger seat of a souped-up street car. You have checked the security of your buckle a second time. And a third. You're white-knuckled to the door handle, even if this true stock car is a veritable wimp compared with the fearsome beasts that race here.

Naturally, you also are trying to look cool and non-plussed. You're fooling no one.

Especially when your chauffeur takes you high and fast into the sweeping turn of this, the best and biggest and most frightening amusement park ride of your life, and casually removes both his hands from the steering wheel as the speedometer reaches triple-digits and G-forces constrict your chest.

You blurt something unintelligible or profane. Or both. The driver cackles with glee.

You have just learned your first physics lesson about Talladega Superspeedway, this 2.66-mile track with towering, daunting Bristol-style turns linked by endless straightaways. To stay on the banking this high, three lanes up, you must be traveling in the neighborhood of 100 mph, or else gravity would regain command, causing the car to topple over. And, at this speed, in this much of a swoop around a corner, there is no need in steering. The car has yielded to centrifugal force. Talladega Superspeedway has had a lifelong, tumultuous affair with the laws of physics.

Once upon a time, it was ballyhooed as "The World's Fastest Speedway." In its infancy, it was so dangerous the regular NASCAR drivers turned away in fear. Its perils have initiated some of the sport's most complex and controversial rules. It has provided dramatic and unpredictable racing. Case in point: In July 1984, there

If a driver moves high or low to make a pass at Talladega, he needs a dancing partner. If no one goes with him, he risks falling to the end of the longest line.

were 68 official lead changes out of 188 laps, and the top nine cars finished one-third of a second apart.

Credit for that the most influential of all of Talladega's laws of physics, "drafting," which affects this place more than any other speedway. It is a quirky phenomenon of aerodynamics and air flow that enables cars running closely nose-to-tail to go faster than a car running on its own. In drafting, the front car can actually go faster because of the "push" from behind; the trailing car is sucked into the draft and can use less throttle, in turn exhausting less fuel.

However, woe be unto the driver who wriggles free of the security of a draft. Play it wrong, and a third-place spot quickly becomes 23rd, back there at the caboose of the Talladega freight train—the most painful of all physics lessons learned.

This place was designed for speed. Daytona, its sister track, was fast. Bill France Sr. wanted Talladega to be even faster. He got it.

The banking is 33 degrees, nearly as precarious as Bristol's bowl. The back stretch is 4,000-feet long, wide enough to run five- and six-wide, should the driver grow that daring. Grandstands reach the entire length of the 4,300-foot front straight, with its trioval configuration. Unique to 'Dega, the start-finish line

Dale Jarrett's pit crew works on his car in this 2001 race. Jarrett won the Winston 500 at Talladega in 1998 and collected a $1 million bonus.

is well down the front stretch, nearly to Turn 1. All the better, Big Bill figured, for his high-falutin' crowd in the few primitive "luxury" boxes originally constructed at that end of the speedway.

It may be the most deceptive speedway of them all. Nowhere are the cars traveling faster; nowhere, when watching a distant corner, do they appear to be moving more slowly, looking like scale-model cars in patient single-file as you follow them not by the numbers on their sides but instead by the bold numbers painted on their roofs.

Talladega Superspeedway—Alabama International Motor Speedway at birth—sits alongside I-20, which connects Birmingham, 45 miles to the west, and Atlanta, 90 miles to the east. Bill Ward, an insurance man from nearby Anniston, broached the idea of building a speedway in Alabama to France, who challenged him to

"find me 2,000 acres and I will." Ward discovered a soybean farm adjacent to an old airstrip the Navy had used for training during World War II. Deals were struck. France got the land, and Talladega got a new airport.

Technically, the area is called "Dry Valley," which rings ironic when the inevitable race-weekend rain comes a-pounding. Local legend has it that the speedway is located on an Indian graveyard, and is cursed. In 1973, driver Bobby Isaac, himself part-Indian, suddenly pulled his car off the track and parked it in the garage. Isaac claimed to hear voices while he was driving. "Something told me to get out of the car," he explained.

It remains a pretty setting, with the backdrop of Mt. Cheaha, Alabama's highest mountain, looming 20 miles beyond Turn 3. The International Motorsports Hall of Fame, a shrine to drivers

The racing at Talledega requires very little movement of the steering wheel; it's about running hard, drafting and letting the force of the banking take you around the track.

from all genres of racing, is on the speedway grounds. Harley-Davidson has a plant near the speedway, and uses it as a test site. The track has undergone a cosmetic makeover, with splashes of red and blue in the grandstands and the 10-lane main entrance was decorated with red and blue stanchions and pennants. A large piece of property across from the track was sheared of vegetation, permitting I-20 travelers a spectacular view of the speedway.

Much of that, alas, doesn't affect a great nucleus of the Talladega fan base. The speedway draws thousands of fans to the endless infield and vast camping areas, and they come to the track for good times as much as for the racing. Many of the drivers hold a warm appreciation for the unpretentious nature of the good ol' boys among the campers.

"This place is definitely one of my favorites," Dale Earnhardt Jr. has said. "Truth be known, me and my crew, on Fridays and Saturdays after practice, will incognito-style get in a rental car and ride through the infield and check out some of the crazy stuff going on in there. It's like a mini-Mardi Gras. They know how to have a good time, I'll tell you that."

Bill France Sr. got his fast track but didn't have any drivers.

The racing always has been tight at Talladega, but the grandstands have grown since this 1970 photo. There are 143,000 seats and plenty of room in the infield, a popular spot.

Talladega was set to open in September 1969. "Chargin' Charlie" Glotzbach won the pole, at 199.466 miles per hour. But there were grave concerns about safety. The fresh asphalt track had yet to be properly "cured." It was breaking up in spots. Tire engineers hadn't been able to come up with a compound to withstand the speed and rugged track. The Professional Drivers' Association, a union organized a month earlier and headed by Richard Petty, decided to boycott the event. Only 13 Winston Cup-style cars, accompanied by 33 lighter Grand Touring automobiles, contested the first race—which went off without an accident and was won by Richard Brickhouse, his lone Winston Cup triumph.

The next year, on March 24, with safer tires and conditions here, Buddy Baker became the first driver to exceed 200 mph on a closed course. Bill Elliott, in 1987, set the Talladega qualifying record at 212.809. It likely will stand forever as the fastest lap in stock car racing—not because of his speed, but because of a terrifying wreck during the race that May.

Bobby Allison, the patriarch of "The Alabama Gang," blew a tire coming through the trioval and went airborne. He soared into the catch-fence. It was miraculous. Another few feet, he'd have sailed

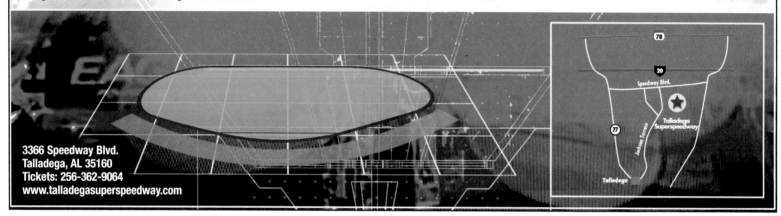

TRACK FACTS

Size: 2.66-mile trioval.
Front straight: 4,300 feet.
Back straight: 4,000 feet.
Banking: 33 degrees in the corners;
2 degrees in the back stretch, 18 degrees in the trioval.

Dale Earnhardt Jr. on Talladega: "You run wherever you can find the draft, and you move around to try to find pockets of air that give your car bursts of speed. Then you can find your place to pass."

3366 Speedway Blvd.
Talladega, AL 35160
Tickets: 256-362-9064
www.talladegasuperspeedway.com

over the fence and into the packed grandstand. But the fence remained almost intact and did its job. Allison walked away only barely shaken from the grisly wreck.

It was one of many events that inexorably linked the Allison clan to Talladega, an hour from its home in the Birmingham suburb of Hueytown. Allison won four races here, and brother Donnie won twice. Davey, Bobby's son, had three Talladega victories, including the 1987 Winston 500, his first NASCAR triumph. But on July 12, 1993, a helicopter Davey was piloting crashed outside the Talladega garage area. He died the next day.

NASCAR officials reacted to Bobby Allison's mishap by deciding

to slow the cars down at Talladega and Daytona, starting in 1988. Restrictor plates, four-inch metal squares, were bolted onto the carburetor intake to restrict air flow. Another science lesson: Oxygen plus fire equals explosion—the fundamental principle of the internal combustion engine.

However, the dearth of power led to controversy—and to coagulated fields and the inability to conjure a quick burst of extra speed for kicking into a "passing gear," to avoid trouble, or to make the dramatic last-lap slingshot moves that had been a Talladega signature for two decades. Drivers approached Talladega with trepidation, knowing one mistake could ignite "The Big One," a multicar, high-speed crash. As

Tony Stewart put it once, "If we can get through to the end of this thing ... roll the car back on the trailer with all the fenders on it, it will be huge."

One of the more memorable Big Ones at Talladega occurred in the summer of 1993. In the melee, Jimmy Horton's car was knocked over the retaining wall and down the embankment on the other side toward a parking area. He emerged uninjured—and with perhaps the greatest quotation in NASCAR history.

"You know you're in trouble," Horton said, "when the first person to get to you after a wreck is carrying a beer."

Ricky Craven's car is kept inside the speedway by the catch-fence between Turns 1 and 2 during a wild ride in a 1996 race at Talladega.

New Era

California
Speedway

Inaugural race:
California 500, June 22, 1997

Stock car racing began in the South. Cars historically were built in Detroit. The most famous race was in Indianapolis.

But it was California that created the "car culture" that spread east across the country as if propelled by El Nino. The whole Baby Boomer generation was weaned on AM radio, hearing songs about the T-bird that daddy would take away and little GTOs, about Sting Rays and XKE's heading into "Dead Man's Curve" and lit-

Fans look on from 92,000 grandstand seats at a track that is 75 feet wide in places and promotes side-by-side racing.

tle deuce coupes.

Those sexy automobiles served a more noble purpose than mere transportation. At least that's what the rest of American youth imagined, tapping a drum-beat on the steering wheels of hand-me-down Fairlanes and Bonnevilles as the music played. They hauled surfboards to the beach. They were status symbols. They were babe magnets. And, when push came to shove, they were a way to flex the muscles, unleash a little testosterone and see who was faster than whom.

With this California car culture, there is little surprise that NASCAR racing has gotten a solid toehold in the state. The only surprise is that it has taken so long to make it a seemingly permanent toehold.

California Speedway, opened in 1997, has given the southern part of the state one of racing's prettiest and fanciest venues, with lush landscaping, palm-tree-lined entrance, the 61 palm trees along the back stretch and a view of the handsomely craggy San Gabriel Mountains in the distance. Mix Bel-Air with Daytona, and this is the product.

In turn, it has given NASCAR entry to the essential media markets of Los Angeles and San Diego. It's the annual opportunity for NASCAR to "go Hollywood," and the race annually draws a generous number of the rich and famous to preen for the cameras and hobnob with the racers.

It's not a California freeway, but traffic heats up on pit road on green-flag stops because cautions often are few.

It is in the town of Fontana, almost equidistant from the ghosts of two now-extinct NASCAR venues, Riverside International Raceway to the south, Ontario Motor Speedway to the west. It is unthinkable to perceive this one going extinct because it was a creation of Roger Penske and is property of the International Speedway Corporation, NASCAR's symbiotic cohort.

This is a $120 million, 2-mile D-shaped oval that has 14-degree banking in the turns, similar to Michigan International Speedway. Says Michael Waltrip, "They call California and Michigan sister tracks. But they look more like stepsisters to me."

So smooth and flowing is this place, with its wide track—a comfortable 75 feet—and sublime corners, "It's just like a really big short track," Waltrip says. "It seems like you just drive down into the corner, let off the gas, let her roll and then get back on the gas." Unlike a short track, California was designed to be conducive to three- and four-wide racing. "The best track I've ever been to," Waltrip's older brother Darrell said after the inaugural race.

Even if California Speedway resembles Michigan, it has borrowed from Indianapolis for one of its most distinctive sites. Standing like a giant exclamation mark on pit lane just opposite the start-finish line is a thin, 146-foot scoring pylon similar to the one that long has been an Indy trademark. It

The tall scoring pylon, modeled after the one at Indianapolis, is an eye-catcher for California fans—as are the San Gabriel Mountains that rise beyond the back stretch.

provides the running order for the fans in the terrace suites, overlooking pit lane in the infield, or for those in the seating that stretches along the front stretch, in the 12,000-plus Speedway Club seats and the luxury boxes atop the main grandstand.

The location is ideal. It is in the elbow of the intersection of I-10 and I-15 in San Bernardino County, northeast of Fontana proper. Los Angeles is a mere 40 miles to the west, with relatively easy access to the speedway. Even easier than driving—sacreligious as that might sound in the "car culture"—fans can leave L.A. via a regularly scheduled Metrolink train that arrives at a station on the speedway grounds. Additionally, there are charter trains

bound for Fontana from more than 40 other stations on race weekends.

The speedway is on the 568-acre site of what had become an environmenal and aesthetic nightmare. In 1942, at the onset of World War II, the Kaiser Steel mill was built, the first of its kind west of the Rockies. It provided the steel for construction of Liberty ships. However, post-war business was slow. On New Year's Eve 1981, the bankrupt Kaiser Steel closed its doors. The plant was abandoned. It grew so dilapidated it was the perfect set for filming part of the original *Terminator* movie in the 1980s. More than 21,000 pounds of hazardous waste had to be moved before

Size: 2-mile D-shaped oval.
Front straight: 2,500 feet.
Back straight: 3,100 feet.
Banking: Turns, 14 degrees; front straight, 11 degrees; back straight, 3 degrees.

Jeremy Mayfield on California: "You have to qualify good so you can stay up front all day. You have to have a car that's balanced so it handles well with a lot of speed."

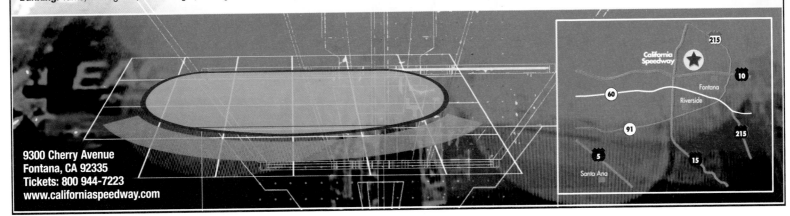

9300 Cherry Avenue
Fontana, CA 92335
Tickets: 800 944-7223
www.californiaspeedway.com

Penske's crew could begin construction on the track.

Fontana is in one of the largest-growing areas in the country as L.A. keeps extended westward toward the desert. It transformed from the steel-mill town into a bedroom community of L.A. and major warehousing and transportation hub. The continuing development of the region was what sounded the death knell for one of the old speedways in the area.

Riverside International Raceway, a road course, became more valuable for developmental purposes than it was for a racetrack and closed in 1988 after hosting 47 Winston Cup events.

Ontario Motor Speedway held nine Winston Cup events, the first in 1971, the last in 1980. So roomy was that track, the first two NASCAR races had 51-car fields, 17 rows three-abreast at the start. Benny Parsons, Bobby Allison and A.J. Foyt each won two races there. It was a 2.5-mile quad oval, mirroring Indianapolis, with a Grand Prix circuit in the infield. Opulence was the keyword for the Ontario creators, who built stands for 200,000 and constructed elegant luxury boxes before they became the norm. They spent $25.5 million to create the vision.

Within nine years, with interest hanging over from a bond issue, Ontario was $42 million in debt. The track was foreclosed, the land sold. Today, a hotel, office complex and outlet mall stand in its place along I-10.

Stock Car Racing magazine said of Ontario in 1971, "Everything is just too shiny, too well organized, too complete, too showy. It is the perfect racing facility dropped out of the sky."

Too perfect to survive.

In its stead is this near-perfect California Speedway.

Chicagolan
Speedway

Inaugural race:
Tropicana 400, July 15, 2001

This toddlin' town, this city of big shoulders, this place had so much in its sports universe.

The most quaint ballpark in baseball. The best basketball player of all time. A ferocity in football that earned decades' worth of its teams the monicker "Monsters of the Midway." Plus all the deep-dish pizza and the blues and the wonderful neighborhoods making up the quiltwork of this city.

What Chicago didn't have for its sports-crazed psyche

There are 75,000 seats and room to add more at the track, which has a bend in both straightaways.

was a major racetrack that wasn't a half-day's drive away.

Then came Chicagoland Speedway. It is Chicago's track—heart, soul ... and very nearly geographically.

"It is not London and Harvard," wrote H.L. Mencken of the city. "It is not Paris and buttermilk. It is American in every chitling and sparerib. It is alive from snout to tail."

That's also Chicagoland Speedway, 45 miles southwest of "The Loop" and downtown Chicago, in the suburban city of Joliet. Alive, snout to tail. Or, at least, front strech to the unique, bowed-out back stretch.

Chicagoland Speedway was built by International Speedway Corporation simultaneously with the creation of Kansas Speedway, to debut in 2001. Ostensibly, the two almost were photocopies of one another. But there are subtle differences. Kansas has its bright pastels, its purples and blues and yellows and its sunflower patterns. Not here. Not in this tough, flinty part of the country. Chicagoland stays loyal to less-flashy blue and black and white in its color scheme. It doesn't have the pretty touches of Kansas. Nor should it. Kansas is the nicely decorated living room with crown molding and textured wallpaper, where you'd better use a coaster before putting your drink on the coffee table. Chicagoland is the family room.

Chicagoland is a 1.5-mile speedway that falls somewhere between being a traditional trioval and a diamond-shaped track. The back stretch bows ever so slightly. Not so much that it

Harvick, crossing the finish line first in the inaugural race, has won the first two Cup events at Chicagoland.

becomes a dramatic bend, like Pocono's "Tunnel Turn" on its back side, but plenty enough to make drivers sit up and take notice as they plow down the banked, 1,700-foot long strip. Engineers also provided more banking in the symmetrical corners than at Kansas—18 degrees here, to 15 at Kansas—and there are two comfortable grooves to promote side-by-side racing.

The 15-story grandstand along the front stretch is nearly a half-mile in length, with seating for 75,000, and leaves plenty of room for expansion.

One driver who quickly took notice of Chicagoland was Jeff Gordon. He was there for a tire test before the first race and gave it a solid thumbs up. "They really have a great racetrack here. It is definitely unique and unlike any other track on the circuit today. I can't find anything I don't like about it," Gordon said then.

Nor could Kevin Harvick likely find anything he didn't like. He won the inaugural Tropicana 400 on July 15, 2001, by a scant .649 seconds. He then made an encore appearance in victory lane the next year—sort of. He nervously gambled on fuel mileage to win the race, and after the ceremonial doughnut-cutting spin in front of the fans, his car conked out, sitting on empty.

Of the nine new tracks on the Winston Cup circuit since 1988, just two drivers have won the first two events at the same track, Harvick here and Tony Stewart at Homestead-Miami (1999-2000). Gordon could find things he didn't like about Harvick in that

The team transporters enter the infield through the tunnel between Turns 3 and 4 early Friday morning on their way to the garage area, where the cars are unloaded.

second race. Harvick daringly swooped below Gordon at one instant, a move Gordon categorized as "stupid." "He thinks it was a stupid move," shrugged Harvick, "and I thought it was pretty cool."

Anyone familiar with every-day Chicago traffic might shudder at the notion of having 75,000 pouring into one place on a Sunday afternoon, but the location is perfect for relatively easy entrance and exit. Chicagoland Speedway is located near both I-55, running north-south, and I-80, running east-west. Various traffic patterns, coded in red, green, blue and yellow, have been designed for fans to follow. Lucky VIPs—like drivers, sponsors

and media—are provided much-coveted passes for a limited-access road, making their arrivals and departures even more simple. Chicago commuters can reach the speedway via rail on the Metra Rock Island line, connecting in downtown Joliet to a bus that will whisk them in.

The $130 million speedway actually brought a return by NASCAR to the area. Always a hotbed for various forms of racing, primarily sports cars, Chicago hosted a pair of NASCAR events in 1956-57 at massive Soldier Field, along the lakefront in downtown Chicago. Andy Granatelli, known to many because of his ties to STP, was then the promoter. Alas, the Bears moved

TRACK FACTS

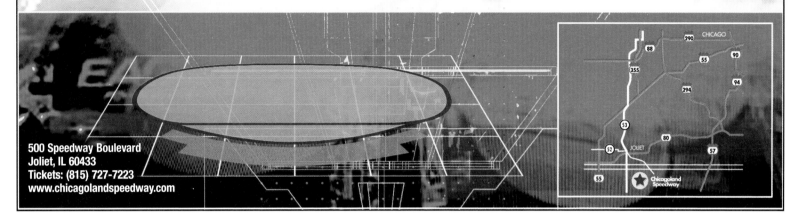

Size: 1.5-mile trioval.
Front straight: 2,400 feet.
Back straight: 1,700 feet.
Banking: Turns, 18 degrees; front straight, 11 degrees; back straight, 5 degrees.

Casey Atwood on Chicagoland: "It's a weird shape. The back straightaway isn't even straight. It's like you're in a full circle all of the time. It reminds me of Las Vegas a little bit, but it has a little bit more banking."

500 Speedway Boulevard
Joliet, IL 60433
Tickets: (815) 727-7223
www.chicagolandspeedway.com

into Soldier Field in 1971, eliminating the racetrack there.

It is a key stronghold in NASCAR's move to be a major national force, making its mark here in the country's second-largest city. The track is owned by a partnership of International Speedway Corporation, Indianapolis Motor Speedway Corporation (primarily the Hulman-George family) and the owners of the adjacent Route 66 Raceway. Chicagoland is the only speedway on the circuit where both a Winston Cup race and dirt-track card happen on the same weekend at the same facility. Route 66 Raceway includes a half-mile dirt oval and a dragstrip with 30,000 seats and 27 luxury boxes, with a long, narrow lake running parallel to it as one pulls into the main entrance.

In addition, Chicagoland was designed to host open-wheel, Indy-type racing. In September 2002, Chicagoland had the closest finish in Indy racing history when Sam Hornish Jr. edged Al Unser Jr. in the Delphi Indy 300 by .0024 seconds.

When Chicagoland opened, the ownership group handed the leadership role to general manager Joie Chitwood III, who departed after two successful years. Chitwood is a scion of the family that launched the famed "Joie Chitwood Thrill Show" in 1944, dazzling generations as an automobile combination of Evel Knievel and the Flying Wallendas, performing all manner of death-defying stunts. "These are trained professionals! Do NOT try them at home!

Joie the Third proved one thing conclusively with his reign at Chicagoland: The Chitwood family could provide wondrous thrills without making cars run on two wheels, turn somersaults or launch through the air.

Homestead
Speedway

Inaugural race:
Pennzoil 400,
November 14, 1999

G ive 'em credit. They found the only bit of undeveloped land left in Florida that wasn't the province of alligators, and they put a racetrack there.

Hey, if they hadn't built a speedway, sooner or later somebody would have put a golf course there, and Florida needs another one of those like it needs another mosquito.

It is Homestead-Miami Speedway, a flat, rather dull 1.5-mile oval down in the heat and humidity of south

Miami

Track officials have done everything possible to give Homestead the look of Miami, from palm trees outside the track wall to the art-deco style of architecture.

Florida. Homestead and Miami are separated by a hyphen in the title, 30 miles on the highway and about 30 million years otherwise. It would be more than a little inaccurate to dream up a mental picture of sailboats bobbing on the waves just beyond the back stretch.

One man's directions to the speedway, only half-joking: "Go south out of Miami and after 30 minutes of nothing, you'll see a house. Turn right at the house. That takes you to the track."

More precisely, it is south on Highway 1, the artery leading out of Miami to the Florida Keys. The surroundings are flat and green, and often marshy, stretching to the Everglades to the west, and even to the visible Miami skyline to the north. It is basically the last stop on the mainland, more country than cosmopolitan.

Still, as a NASCAR man says, "They've done everything they can to give it a South Florida sensation."

The retaining walls are painted teal, apparently the official color of Florida. Palm trees loom outside the wall. There is an art-deco touch to the architecture. It is a pretty place, a bit of South Beach sitting near the Everglades. They've apparently

Stewart (20) won the first two Winston Cup races at Homestead-Miami, but his 18th-place finish there in 2002 was even better—it clinched his first Cup championship.

done everything but plant fake pink flamingos along pit road to provide the Florida feel.

Even the logo accomplishes that.

The word "Homestead" rests atop "Miami," both in blue ink. They are propped against a palm tree. It is teal. Naturally. Both the words and the tree have a perceptible lean to them. Perhaps they are merely swaying in a gentle breeze. Perhaps they are being sucked up in the draft of a speeding racecar. Perhaps it is the beginnings of a hurricane.

To a great extent, Homestead-Miami Speedway symbolizes the area's resiliency as much as its growth. Hurricane Andrew, one of the nation's most devastating storms, ravaged Homestead in the summer of 1992.

Andrew destroyed 80 percent of the homes. Nearly a third of the city's 26,700 left to start afresh elsewhere. The storm did an estimated $20 billion to $30 billion in damage to South Florida. The land on which the speedway sits is near the Homestead Air Force Base, on an old potato field.

In the aftermath of Andrew, racing entrepreneur Ralph Sanchez met with Homestead city officials to propose a speedway to revitalize the area. Ground was broken on August 24,

1993, a year after hurricane struck. Of Sanchez, an admiring CART president Chris Pook said at a 2002 news conference, "He is motorsports in South Florida. Homestead would not be where it is if it wasn't for Ralph. He deserves every bit of credit in my book for what goes on in South Florida, and motor racing in general owes a lot to Ralph Sanchez."

Sanchez, a Cuban immigrant, built the speedway on 434 acres with the assistance of $11 million in hotel taxes and with the aid of millionaire Wayne Huizenga, who has owned the Florida Marlins, Miami Dolphins and much of the Blockbuster movie rental empire. Enlisted as part of of the grand opening ceremonies, Dale Jarrett gushed, "They took a place that was devastated a few years ago, and when people get there and see the job they have done, they're going to be really pleased."

The track, which has 72,000 grandstand seats, was given a face-lift in 1997, including some fresh, bright colors to its structures, but it still has had problems selling out races.

Sanchez had been promoting the Miami Grand Prix at Tamiami Park and, later, on the streets of downtown Miami since the early 1980s. He moved the Grand Prix, for CART racing, to Homestead, and acquired a Busch Series race. The Busch Series met with tragedy. John Nemechek, younger brother of Winston Cup driver Joe Nemechek, was killed in March 1997.

That accident, and a cacophony of complaints from drivers, led to drastic changes. Drivers long wailed about the flat track, which inhibits passing, and about the square-cornered turns. And—let's be honest—another catalyst for change was the opportunity to land a Winston Cup race.

Much as someone who is selling a home will invest in a fresh coat of paint and attractive landscaping to make it more attractive to buyers, Sanchez and Co. invested $8.2 million into this track in 1997,

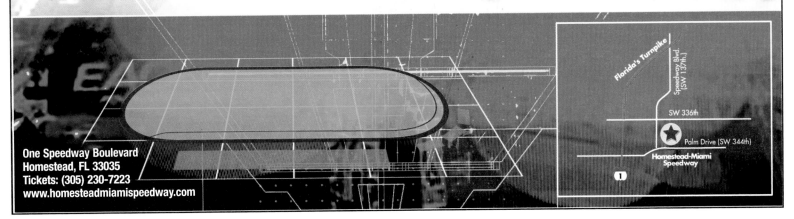

TRACK FACTS

Size: 1.5-mile oval.
Front straight: 1,760 feet.
Back straight: 1,760 feet.
Banking: Turns, 6 degrees; front and back straights, 3 degrees.

Jeff Gordon on Homestead: "It has extremely flat corners but real wide sweeping corners. You see guys sucking their cars down to the ground with shocks and springs and doing some crazy stuff. It's because it's a big, fat, smooth racetrack, but it's also flat."

One Speedway Boulevard
Homestead, FL 33035
Tickets: (305) 230-7223
www.homesteadmiamispeedway.com

turning what had been called a "quad-oval" into a more symmetrical oval. Ultimately, it made it attractive for Winston Cup racing—and as another piece of property for International Speedway Corporation to purchase, which it did in 1998.

Hindsight being 20-20, what also should have been done was to use the renovation opportunity to put some more significant banking in the turns than the-less-even-than-Indy 6 degrees. The track typically does not offer scintillating racing because it essentially remains one lane with single-file racing. Fans seem to recognize that. After a year-long "Road To Miami" P.R. blitz that promoted three NASCAR titles—Winston Cup, Busch and Craftsman truck series—to be determined there in 2002, track officials were scrambling last-minute to sell tickets despite the relatively modest 72,000 capacity.

But don't try to convince Tony Stewart this place isn't exciting. He won the first two Winston Cup events at Homestead-Miami. Perhaps it was his IndyCar experience—he was the 1997 Indy Racing League champ before hopping to NASCAR—that made him so imposing on the flat track.

Even still, those two first-place finishes were nothing compared with the day Stewart finished a meager 18th here. That was the November afternoon in 2002 when he wrapped up the Winston Cup championship, the bad-boy image melting away in a calvacade of confetti and smiles. The points chase had come down to this final race of the year, and an eventual 38-point cushion over hard-charging Mark Martin. So, was that a gentle breeze or a hurricane blowing the Homestead-Miami logo and the teal palm tree sideways—or was it a heavy sigh of relief from Tony Stewart?

Kansas Speedway

Inaugural race:
Protection One 400,
September 30, 2001

The hottest ticket in motorsports? How about a seat high above the start-finish line at Daytona? How about a VIP seat at Indianapolis? How about an aisle seat overlooking the carnage at Bristol?

Turns out the hottest ticket may not even be for a seat.

Kansas Speedway, which opened for business in 2001, proudly boasts the "Fan Walk," a magical tour that quickly captivated the patrons at this 1.5-mile tri-oval out in the pretty coun-

The infield at Kansas Speedway is fan friendly, with easy access to hospitality events and souvenirs.

tryside west of Kansas City. "Fan Walk" provides a leisurely stroll through the garage area, with close-up looks at the inner-workings of the sport. It's a trip to the zoo—but smells better. Tickets are gobbled up quickly.

Fans enter from outside Turn 1 and travel through a kaliedesopic 450-foot tunnel full of colored lights into the infield. Though a fence separates them from the working area, large slots have been placed in the fence to allow autograph-seekers to pass mementoes through to drivers for their signatures. "Fan Walk" meanders past the NASCAR inspection area, which has clear doors to permit the spectactors to watch the process. At various times, NASCAR officials are outfitted with microphones to explain the proceedings and answer questions.

At other moments, there might be a concert. Or a live TV broadcast. Or jugglers. Or contests in which fans can pretend to be NASCAR crew members changing tires. Replica racecars and exotic automobiles are on display. It is a carnival atmosphere. And though many tracks extend themselves to cater to the upper-class swells with ritzy suites and exclusive hospitality villages, Kansas has put an emphasis on the every-day fan.

That extends to the grandstands themselves, with an initial con-

Most fans aren't allowed in the work areas, but many waited and hoped for an autograph at the September 2002 race.

struction of 78,000 seats along the front stretch and through Turn 1. (It was designed eventually to have 150,000 seats.) The track is sunk into a bowl so that fans even on the bottom row can see the entire track. As a result, the concourse is street level. No breathstealing, beverage-spilling hike up 65 rows to the top of the grandstands. Half of the stands are below the concourse, the other half above.

There also is a history lesson of sorts. Homage is paid to Kansas's cousins, with streets meandering through the 1,200-acre property that are named for Daytona, Talladega, Michigan and other speedways.

Aesthic value is a priority here. Lesa France Kennedy, executive vice president of International Speedway Corporation and daughter of Bill France Jr., was a driving force in the completion of Kansas Speedway. She made sure it had some almost fanciful bits of decoration. Black and white are the traditional colors of racing, with the famous checkered flag, but Kennedy realized that we live in a technicolor world.

The tops of the garages and the garage doors are blue. The inspection garages have yellow overhangs. There are purples and yellows and greens and blues everywhere. Even some of the signage has colorful sprinkles, like confetti. As a speedway official once put it, proudly, "With more children, more

Pit stops, like this one by Dale Earnhardt Jr. in the September 2002 race, are key at Kansas because track position can be gained more easily here than on the speedway.

families, more women, it's really got to look like Disneyland now."

It is, according to the slogan, "The Track That Will Blow You Away."

And, apparently, that's not merely a fan's perspective.

"This," pronounced Rusty Wallace after the second event here, "is a great venue to have Winston Cup racing at."

Kansas Speedway fits the same template as many of the newer tracks, at a mile and a half and with the trioval shape to permit better front-stretch vistas for the fans. It is perfectly symetrical,

with banked turns at either end at 15 degrees. The front trioval also is relatively steeply banked, though the back is virtually flat. At 55 feet wide, the track is forgiving.

However, drivers complained in the inaugural event, the Protection One 400 in September 2001, that there was just one consistent racing groove. It was especially groovy for Jeff Gordon, who won by .413 seconds over Ryan Newman. Gordon also won the first Brickyard 400 and the first race at California Speedway.

Kansas improved some the second time around and seems cer-

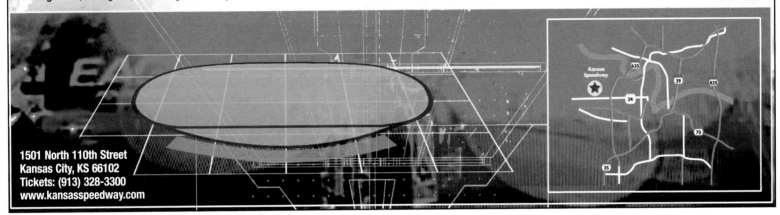

TRACK FACTS

Size: 1.5-mile trioval.
Front straight: 2,721 feet.
Back straight: 2,207 feet.
Banking: Turns, 15 degrees; front straight, 10.4 degrees; back straight, 5 degrees.

Jeff Gordon on Kansas: "Any track where it's hard to pass, where there's not two- or three-wide racing you're going to see guys use their bumpers. Heck, we're seeing it at Daytona and Talladega now, so it doesn't surprise me to see it here."

1501 North 110th Street
Kansas City, KS 66102
Tickets: (913) 328-3300
www.kansasspeedway.com

tain to get even better as the track matures, tire compounds are perfected and teams learn more. "We can race side-by-side more," Johnny Benson said. "Plus it makes it more of a challenge for the teams. Now car setup and the driver become more important."

Auto racing has long been popular in the Midwest. Some of NASCAR's best drivers—Wallace, Mark Martin, Ken Schrader—grew up racing in these parts. This was a natural place for ISC to plant another flag for its empire. Indeed, when tickets went on sale for the inaugural event, 60,000 phone calls were fielded the first week with ticket requests and questions.

The speedway is 15 miles from downtown Kansas City, on the opposite end of the city from the handsome Truman Sports Complex, with Arrowhead Stadium for the Chiefs and Royals Stadium for the city's baseball club. From the top row of the stands, one can see the Kansas City skyline. The speedway is at the junction of

Interstate 70 and Interstate 435, and speedway officials are quick to brag about the efficient traffic flow the freeways allow.

The surrounding area still is a green, hilly countryside; it's still a few miles before the hills recede into the long, flat, endless plains. It is brightened with millions of happy smiles from wild sunflowers.

Kansas Speedway has brought a financial boon to Wyandotte County, which heretofore didn't even have a movie theater. It did, at one point, host a greyhound racing venue, but that went under in the 1990s without luring any significant development.

Things changed when a bit faster animal started racing around. A minor league baseball team moved into town. Malls, restaurants, shops and even a 38,000-square foot indoor water park have been built.

All that, with a speedway as the catalyst.

All that ... why it's enough to blow you away.

Las Vegas
Motor Speedway

Nickname:
The Diamond in the Desert

Inaugural race:
Las Vegas 400, March 1, 1998

It had to happen. Las Vegas was swaying into the mainstream of America. The gangsters were fading from the scene. The Rat Pack was dead. Sammy and Frank and Dino were replaced by Wayne Newton and tiger-tamers. Hotels were building wave pools and roller coasters. Video games in which 12-year-old boys could annihilate alien invaders were becoming as important as slot machines.

And NASCAR was swaying

into the mainstream. NASCAR was looking for venues where there was more neon besides the Hardee's opening at 5 a.m. with fresh biscuits for the race crowd.

It was inevitable Las Vegas and NASCAR would collide.

It was inevitable, being Las Vegas, that excess prevailed. A 1,500-acre, $200 million racing equivalent to the Bellagio or Caesar's Palace or the MGM Grand sprang up like some lavish steel and concrete oasis in the desert. And that the Las Vegas Motor Speedway offered one of the top five paydays on the Winston Cup circuit for the race winner made drivers and car owners giddy with delight.

Not only was a flat, 1.5-mile asphalt trioval created, with 126,000 grandstand seats, but satellite tracks were built on the property. The "Bullring," a three-eighths mile paved short track.

A half-mile dirt oval. A paved Legends car track. A go-kart track. An off-road motorcross circuit. A 17-turn road course inside the main speedway. A drag strip, with 20,000 seats and VIP boxes.

Hey, you wouldn't build a casino in Las Vegas where you could play only blackjack, right? You've got to have roulette and craps and the clang-clang-clang of a gazillion slot machines. So, you can't just build one track.

When they built the one centerpiece track, they built a gem. "Diamond in the Desert," they call it.

The seating area wraps around the front stretch tri-oval, reaching all the way around beyond Turn 3 and into the Backstretch Brandstand, with the Sheep Range mountains looming over its shoulder. More than 100 VIP boxes overlook the front stretch.

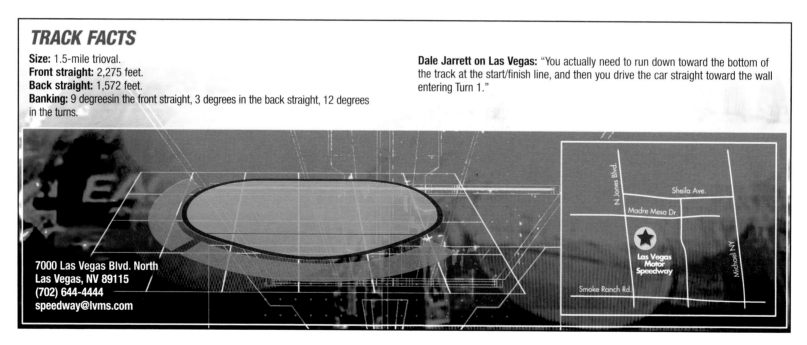

TRACK FACTS

Size: 1.5-mile trioval.
Front straight: 2,275 feet.
Back straight: 1,572 feet.
Banking: 9 degreesin the front straight, 3 degrees in the back straight, 12 degrees in the turns.

Dale Jarrett on Las Vegas: "You actually need to run down toward the bottom of the track at the start/finish line, and then you drive the car straight toward the wall entering Turn 1."

7000 Las Vegas Blvd. North
Las Vegas, NV 89115
(702) 644-4444
speedway@lvms.com

N Jones Blvd
Sheila Ave.
Madre Mesa Dr.
Las Vegas Motor Speedway
Michael NY
Smoke Ranch Rd.

Because its wraparound grandstands provide a view of racing and the mountains, Las Vegas is known as the "Diamond in the Desert."

The speedway sits 8 miles north of downtown Las Vegas—or three hours in postrace traffic—adjacent to Nellis Air Force Base. (Coincidences: The old Riverside International Raceway also was next to an Air Force base, and Talladega Superspeedway is built on the site of an old air base.) The Vegas back stretch is called the "Nellis Straightaway" because it runs parallel to the runways at Nellis, where the famed Thunderbirds are based, as well as the Air Warfare Center. Next door is a factory where Carroll Shelby's Cobras are built, with a museum featuring those memorable speedsters.

When the speedway was built, it wasn't merely to capitalize on the extravagance of Vegas visitors and the relative affluence of the community to support the facility. It wasn't merely to hedge bets that NASCAR fans would flock to the city, with its myriad attractions even more intoxicating than the smell of fuel and burning tires. It won that bet.

Fans come cross-country in droves. It is cars by day, cards by night. Maybe a side trip to Boulder Dam or the Grand Canyon. The decadence and sensory overload that is Vegas, with shows and casinos, saloons and fine restaurants, B-list comics and Elvis impersonators, are a wonderful distraction from the sleepy, small-town Southern roots of the sport.

The track's hallmark features are the mountains that provide a breathtaking backdrop and a racing surface that is flat, smooth and unusually wide.

The speedway developers didn't dive into this project without doing their homework. They visited tracks all over the world for several years. They learned, they said later, that fans had three priorities: good access roads, restrooms and hotel rooms.

Two out of three—the last two—isn't bad.

"I swear, when they built (it) somebody just kept going out there and saying, 'Make it a little wider, a little wider. Now, make it perfectly smooth,'" Jeff Burton says. "So you've got a perfectly smooth, really wide racetrack. That should give you all the space and lanes that you need."

It is a trioval, mimicking in design most of the newly constructed tracks that provide better sightlines for fans in the front-stretch stands. The turns have 12-degree banking, slightly flatter than, say, Charlotte and Kansas, which it resembles in shape. Though they are banked the same, Turns 2 and 4 have subtle differences, and drivers must be wary of that. With the trioval and the long turns, drivers almost constantly are cranking the steering wheel to the left, except for the 1,572-foot back stretch. It requires a smooth line and a lot of patience. It essentially is a one-groove track.

After Mark Martin won the first Winston Cup race at Vegas on March 1, 1998, Roush Racing teammate Burton followed by winning the next two. Welcome to Roush Roulette. Jeff Gordon finally broke the spell, coming from 24th starting spot to win in 2001, the fourth Winston Cup event at Vegas.

NASCAR was proceeded in the desert by other circuits. The Indy Racing League christened the speedway with the Las Vegas 500 in 1996, followed soon by the World of Outlaws, then the Winston Cup circuit.

However, Las Vegas has a deep history in racing. Not far from this site, Craig Road Speedway, a quarter-mile paved oval, operated from 1965 through 1982. It was a learning ground for many Midwesterners and West Coast drivers who ultimately headed for Winston Cup. Martin raced at Craig Road Speedway. So did Ernie Irvan, Derrike Cope and Dick Trickle.

What would racing in Las Vegas be without showgirls? Though the racing isn't much different, the setting—with shows, casinos and saloons—is a departure from the sport's Southern roots.

Las Vegas even spawned its own favorite son for the NASCAR circuit, the angular youngster Kurt Busch, the 2001 Winston Cup Rookie of the Year runner-up to Kevin Harvick. Busch began racing in dwarf cars at age 14 at Pahrump Valley Speedway, a quarter-mile clay track in the desert west of Las Vegas Speedway.

In 1999, the precocious Busch won a try-out of sorts in which team owner Jack Roush auditioned a number of young, inexperienced drivers for a spot in his empire. Roush put them in the same car and had the car tweaked to be especially challenging. He studied how drivers communicated their needs to crew chiefs and how they responded to the difficulty. He even had them perform mock media interviews to judge their skills in public relations.

"He tripped the light fantastic," Roush recalled of Busch's audition. Could be, before it's all said and done with his career, Kurt Busch might be the best Vegas jackpot Roush Racing ever hit.

Texas

Motor Speedway

Inaugural race:
Interstate Batteries 500
April 6, 1997

Y ou had to know it
would happen.
    If someone were
going to build a racetrack in
Texas, it had to be bigger
and better and faster and
brassier than all the rest.
Texas wouldn't settle for
anything else.
    And if they had a little
controversy and stubbor-
ness to go along with it,
well, podner, then so be it.
And some bluster and brag-
gadocio. It's all the better
for the state that inspired
the Ewings, hosts the Cow-

boys and gave birth to LBJ.

Texas Motor Speedway is indeed a palatial monument to speed and excess. It is a 1.5-mile D-shaped oval, with steep banking, that rests just north of Fort Worth in the massive "Metroplex."

It is, in many ways, typical of the tracks in the Bruton Smith Speedway Motorsports Inc. chain that also operates in Charlotte, Atlanta and Las Vegas, among others. It follows much the same blueprint in size and shape. It has its touches of architectural grandeur and landscaping. There are seven enormous flower beds with 16,000 plants; the track is ringed by 225 flags of various racing lineage. It has its luxuries and extras. Outside Turn 1 is the $35 million Speedway Club, with its ballroom that seats 1,000, much like Charlotte's club. Adjacent to that is the Lone Star Tower, a 10-story building. Office space, rented by local corporations, is on the first through fourth floors. Luxury condos, 76 units ranging from 1,000 to 2,000 square feet and selling for upwards of a half-million dollars, are on floors five through 10.

At the condos' feet is a racetrack that is fast. Dangerously fast. Controversially fast. Fast enough to have prompted Jeff

The track wasn't without problems early; millions were spent to rework the drainage system and the entrances and exits to the turns.

Burton to complain, "I hate the track, as fast as it is, (and) I wish it didn't have to be that way."

Eddie Gossage, the track's general manager, once shrugged, "I don't think there's any question some controversy can be your friend, if it's not contrived." And as much as may be contrived at SMI's speedways, the biggest controversy to hit Texas Motor Speedway was legit. From the outset, Indy-style cars almost were going supersonic. Tony Stewart, the 2002 Winston Cup champ, still was driving open-wheel cars and was the first driver to surpass 200 mph at Texas, in testing in February 1997.

In April 2001, CART cancelled its Firestone Firehawk 600 at Texas two hours before the race was to begin. Doctors and race officials agreed that drivers were enduring excessive G-forces, which led to vertigo-like symptoms for some during their practices.

That came four years after the inaugural Indy Racing League event here in which Arie Luyendyk was declared the winner the day after the race after he filed a protest. Race officials agreed that the speedway's malfunctioning timing and scoring equipment erroneously had given Billy Boat the win.

NASCAR had an equally difficult debut. On April 6, 1997, 13 cars crashed on the first lap of the first Winston Cup race. The next year, there was water seepage that hampered practice and qualifying.

Speedway officials answered by reconstructing the track's draining system and, more dramatically, making changes to the entrances and exits to the turns. The turns initially were dual-banked, at 24 degrees at the top, 8 degrees on the bottom section. The revamping, at a price tag of $4 million, made it easier for cars to transition from the steeper banks into the flat sections, and vice versa.

It also made the track faster.

Good for Texas and its boasts. Scary for the drivers.

This is NASCAR's second foray into the state. Texas World Speedway, a two-mile, high-banked oval, was built in 1969 on the plains near College Station, home to Texas A&M. The speedway included another oval inside the track, plus road courses of varying lengths. It was a superspeedway the magnitude of Daytona, Talladega and Michigan when it opened.

It could boast one enviable record: The 1979 NASCAR race ran 396 laps before its first caution, and that only for two laps before going green for the final two of 400 laps. The next year, there was nary a caution. That's four miles of caution out of 800 miles. However, the track didn't draw well, and the original owners feuded with the France family. By 1981, it vanished from the schedule.

Clearly, though, Texas was a lucrative marketplace the sport couldn't ignore.

As this track has evolved, it has added more facets and more lore. Lil' Texas Motor Speedway, a paved oval, and Texas Motor Speedway dirt track are outside the back stretch, the latter sit-

The condos and suites above Turn 1 are similar to those at Charlotte.

TRACK FACTS

Size: 1.5-mile D-shaped oval.
Front straight: 2,250 feet.
Back straight: 1,330 feet.
Banking: Turns, 24 degrees; front and back straightaways, 5 degrees.

Dale Earnhardt Jr. on Texas: "It's one of our best tracks. Ever since we started going there in the Busch Series, it has been a track that has been easy for me to drive. I guess I have a good feel for what the car needs as far as its attitude into and off the corners."

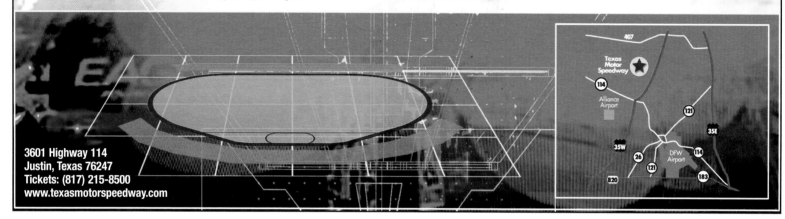

3601 Highway 114
Justin, Texas 76247
Tickets: (817) 215-8500
www.texasmotorspeedway.com

ting adjacent to a small lake. As if to enhance the lore, the side streets on track property are named for drivers. After exiting I-35 on Dale Earnhardt Way, there is Victory Circle, with various spokes like Andretti Avenue, Waltrip Way, Parsons Lane and Burton Boulevard leading to parking areas, and Lone Star Circle that is the collar just outside the speedway.

Lore got a pretty big boost again when Dale Earnhardt Jr. collected his inaugural Busch Series win (April 4, 1998) and Winston Cup win (April 2, 2000) here. The latter came in his 12th race on the circuit, and he told reporters later what his team owner said to him in victory lane. "He told me he loved me and then he said he just wanted to make sure I took the time to enjoy this and realize what we accomplished today." The car owner was his father, Dale Earnhardt, who 10 months later was killed at Daytona.

By the new millennium, Texas Motor Speedway had begun to outgrow many of its controversies. Drivers had become more accustomed to the place. Traffic problems, among the worst the sport ever endured, were alleviated.

There was, typical of Texans, one final, massive frontier left to tackle. In October 2002, Gossage made a proposal. They would modify an area in the infield into a football field. The Texas-Oklahoma game, played annually in front of 75,000 at the Texas Fairgrounds, could move to Texas Motor Speedway. The attendance could double.

Naturally, if that ever came about, Texas could boast the largest college football crowd in history. People sat up and took notice at the idea. Racing is one thing. Now they were talking football in Texas. Now they really could put this speedway to good use.

Dale Earnhardt Jr. (8) got his first Winston Cup win at Texas on April 2, 2000, and also recorded his first Busch Series win here, much to the delight of more than 150,000 fans.

Road Courses

Infineon Raceway

Also known as:

Sears Point Raceway

Inaugural race:

Banquet 300, June 11, 1989

So, what would *The Wine Spectator*, that highly respected Bible of wine connisseurs, have to say about this proud, legendary Napa/Sonoma product?

To steal some of the magazine's exuberant adjectives, it might be described as "rich, complex, yet delicate and sharply focused." Or "a sense of elegance and finesse." Or "silky and juicy." Or, a popular one, "seductive."

These adjectives are not

directed toward wine in this instance. They are directed toward a vintage racetrack that sprawls across an undulating, golden piece of property in the California wine country.

Infineon Speedway, nee Sears Point Raceway, has indeed seduced thousands of race fans in the northern California area because of the track's unique natural beauty and the scintillating brand of racing that the Winston Cup circuit's annual stop provides.

Infineon is 30 miles north of San Francisco. It stands almost as the gateway to Wine Country. That way to Glen Ellen. This way to Sonoma. Keep going that way to Napa. Turn left into that gate for racing thrills.

How about more adjectives?

"Uncommon depth and complexity." It was used by *The Wine Spectator* to describe a lush new Pinot Noir ... but fits perfectly the task of manuevering the Infineon course.

It is a narrow track that demands precise shifting and steering. As Bobby Labonte once related, having asked for advice from his brother Terry on how to drive here, "He said I had to make sure to keep the car on the racing surface and not get off into the gravel. Saying it and doing it are two different things."

It is a two-mile road course, rising dramatically after the start-

Getting on the throttle in the corners at Infineon often means racing with only three—and sometimes two—wheels on the pavement.

finish line to scale the side of a steep hill. In more simple times, this space was popular with fans who would find a comfy place on the slope to stretch out a blanket and unpack a picnic basket.

Now, to accommodate the many more fans who have been seduced by the place, terrace grandstands were placed along the hillside as the 21st century rolled around, as well as on a reconfigured Turn 7. Open spaces where fans used to spread out blankets and unpack picnic lunches, perhaps with a smuggled-in bottle of the local product, had become prime seats. A shuttle system was put in place to deliver spectators to their seats.

Because the turns are so tight and straightaways short, "It's pretty much follow the leader," Rusty Wallace has said. Infineon is a vivid contrast to the other road course on the NASCAR schedule, Watkins Glen, in central New York. The Glen has longer straights, more subtle corners and is more conducive to passing. Drivers have noted Watkins Glen is a superspeedway of road courses, Infineon a short track of road courses.

In 1999, the route for Winston Cup cars at Infineon was drastically changed, shortened by more than a half-mile. It made the track more spectator-friendly, and because more laps were added,

TRACK FACTS

Size: 2.0-mile road course.
Turns: 11, with varying lengths and
degree of banking.
The Chute: 890 feet, 2.8 degrees.

Jeff Gordon on running at Infineon: "You have to attack the track. There's nowhere
you can be more aggressive than a road course. A successful driver here is a guy
who is comfortable with his shifting and braking points and knows he can get more
aggressive."

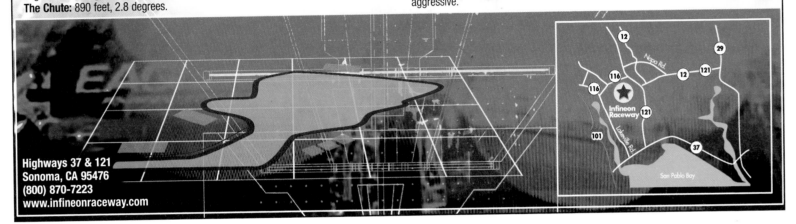

Highways 37 & 121
Sonoma, CA 95476
(800) 870-7223
www.infineonraceway.com

the competitive strategy was tweaked. After the start-finish line, in the shadow of the ritzy grandstand tower and its VIP seats, there is a little crook to the left, then a sweeping left as cars scale the hill, leading to a 70-degree right.

Rather than cascading back down the hill and going through the famed "Carousel," the reconfiguration connects the old Turn 4 to what was once a hairpin Turn 7 with a long straightaway. Turn 7 is a 90-degree right that provides a dramatic passing area, as does the straight leading into it. As the cars return home, there is one more scrambling passing area, in the final corner, where drivers dice as tightly inside as possible, rubbing the inside pylons the way slalom skiers brush against the gate poles on a snowy mountain.

Track officials consulted a number of drivers before the changes. Some drivers were placed in computer simulators and asked to navigate three proposed layouts.

Perhaps that is appropriate for the high-tech nature of northern California and for a speedway that acquired, in 2002, the corporate title of Infineon, a German-based computer chip company. With the naming rights purchased for $35 million through 2012, perhaps it will add consistency to a speedway that has a history full of transition. Sears Point has swapped hands like a bad penny, going from the folks who invented "The Beverly Hillbillies" to a big-name driver to, ultimately, the inimitable Bruton Smith, who collects speedways the way a 12-year-old collects baseball cards.

Inactivity certainly won't be a problem. Something is happening at Infineon 50 weeks out of the year, whether it is the annual NASCAR event, a drag race, go-kart competitions or driving schools.

The original naming rights for the area were for Franklin Sears,

a Missourian who moved West with a rifle, a mule and $1.50. After earning fame as a hero in the U.S.-Mexican war, he settled on 600 acres south of Sonoma to work as a blacksmith and a rancher in 1851. More than 100 years later, a pair of Marin County men had the idea to develop Sears Point for a racetrack. Ground was broken, and within four months, December 1, 1968, the first race was held here. Filmways Corporation, a major Hollywood studio that cranked out some of the 1960s top sitcoms, bought Sears Point in 1969 for $4.5 million only to shut it down in less than two years as a tax shelter, having lost $300,000. Three years later, two local men agreed to lease the track from Filmways, and the famed Bob Bondurant announced he would move his driving school here. Bondurant eventually bought out Filmways, but the track remained under unsettled ownership for nearly two decades before Smith galloped to the rescue in 1996. Much as Smith did with other tracks, Sears Point suddenly was flooded with an influx of capital that produced dramatic improvements. For instance, the $35 million plan in 2001 that added the hillside terrace seats, permanent garages and the changes in Turn 7, transforming it from a remote, seldom-seen corner into a hub of spectator activity. Six to seven million cubic yards of dirt were moved during all the reconfiguration.

Now, that's a bit of farming that leaves even those at the area wineries astounded. But there is one thing the road course and the wineries have in common: It sure seems like Infineon Raceway just gets better with time.

"You're never going straight. You're always turning," says Wally Dallenbach of Infineon's curvy layout. "If you just touch anybody, you're probably going to run them off the track."

Watkins Glen

International

Inaugural race:
The Glen, August 4, 1957

Right. Right. Left. Right. Right. Left. Left. Right. Right. Left. Right.

That is not some combination of boxing punches, or complex, ankle-twisting instructions at the Arthur Murray Dance School.

It is instead the snaky, demanding route around Watkins Glen International, the world-renowned speedway that spreads atop a New York mountain like the most twisted, abstract game of connect-the-dots you've ever seen.

This historic layout almost reminds one of some glamorous Hollywood movie siren of the 1950s. It was involved in one of racing's most thrilling eras, survived bankruptcy, underwent countless face-lifts and somehow emerged decades later once again as a regal, enduring star.

The Glen is the ultimate challenge as a road course, not merely because of its 11 turns. It has a half-mile straightaway between Turns 4 and 5, and the 2,150-foot front stretch is a downhill line past towering grandstands, ending in an abrupt right turn that defies geometry and gravity, and often the laws of traffic courtesy.

With the long straights, cars race upward of 180 miles per hour. Engines need the power generated on superspeedways, yet the corners require the precise chassis set-ups and durable brakes needed at a Martinsville or Richmond.

The Glen also demands total concentration on a driver's part.

But, ironically, Kyle Petty once suggested, it doesn't demand an impeccable performance.

"The nice thing about a road course is you don't have to be perfect. In fact, I don't think you can be perfect," Petty said. "No matter how quick a lap you run, you can always look back and think, 'Man, if I had hit this mark a little better,' or 'If I had gotten through this turn a little tighter.' "

The incessant right-left-right business at The Glen has a secondary bit of complication. Pit road runs parallel to the front stretch on the right. On every other track, the pits are on the left. This necessitates fuel input valves on the right rear fenders rather than left. It can throw off the chaotic ballet of a pit stop. Inevitably, a crew or two will wind up stumbling and confused when instinct takes over, leaving them red-faced.

Nothing, however, like the embarrassment endured by NBC tele-

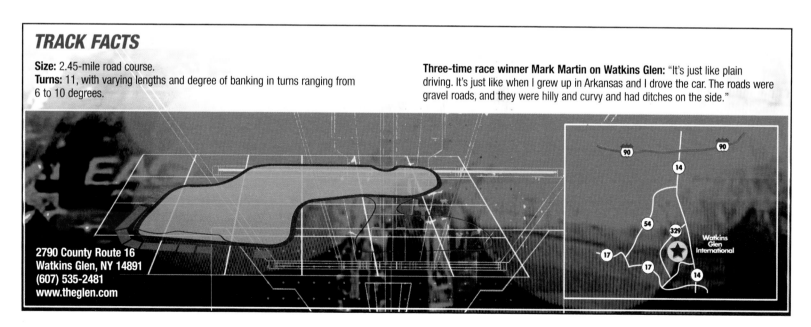

TRACK FACTS

Size: 2.45-mile road course.
Turns: 11, with varying lengths and degree of banking in turns ranging from 6 to 10 degrees.

Three-time race winner Mark Martin on Watkins Glen: "It's just like plain driving. It's just like when I grew up in Arkansas and I drove the car. The roads were gravel roads, and they were hilly and curvy and had ditches on the side."

2790 County Route 16
Watkins Glen, NY 14891
(607) 535-2481
www.theglen.com

In addition to NASCAR's Winston Cup, The Glen has been a regular stop on a number of other series' schedules.

vision in 2001. Robby Gordon was leading at The Glen that day when a telemetry box inside his car used by the network caught fire. Before the fire could be extinguished, so were Gordon's chances. The following August, the Richard Childress Racing team tongue-in-cheek presented NBC with an invoice for $1,782,173, figuring a loss of race winnings coupled with punitive damages for pain and suffering. Additionally, NBC was presented a scorched die-cast model version of Gordon's Chevrolet.

The Glen layout is adjustable. For NASCAR Winston Cup races, the course is 2.45 miles—the "long course" goes 3.45 miles—across a rolling, forested piece of property often shrouded by mountain fog mixed with smoke from campfires and barbecue grills. Because of the vastness of the property encircled by the track, The Glen provides the most back-to-nature infield camping in the sport.

The gnarly Turn 1 is a perfect introduction to The Glen. Cars wrestle for inside position and it is essential to brake at just the right moment to avoid losing too much momentum—or to avoid taking too much momentum into the run-off area and barriers beyond. The "esses," Turns 2, 3 and 4, lead into the long back straight. The track was reconfigured at the end of the straight after 1991, when J.D. McDuffie was killed after failing to negotiate the steep, righthanded Turn 5—"The Loop"—and slammed into the barrier. A slight chicane with right and left turns was added to slow the cars.

Coming out of The Loop, another long straight looms before a sharp left and the last big bending right turn, where grandstand spectators see cars suddenly appearing over a distant horizon, underneath a pedestrian bridge, and come skidding violently to

the left side before regaining their composure for the drag race downhill on the front.

It is actually the fourth incarnation of a race course here. In 1948, a 6.6-mile sports-car course was designed on paved, dirt and gravel roads throughout The Glen, encompassing some of the city streets. One of the participants in the first event was Charles Addams, a man more widely known for his ghoulish cartoons—*The Addams Family*—than his driving skills.

Tragedy brought on the construction of a new course outside town in 1953 after 13 spectators were injured, one fatally, when a racer lost control in downtown Watkins Glen. A more permanent paved course was built in 1956. It became host to a NASCAR event in 1957—won by Buck Baker—and the U.S. Grand Prix made The Glen its home for 19 years. In 1981, Watkins Glen went bankrupt, but after sitting dormant two years, it was saved by the Corning Glass Company, based in nearby Corning, N.Y. NASCAR returned in 1986—Tim Richmond won—and the organization solidified The Glen's future when sister company International Speedway Corporation bought it in 1997.

Watkins Glen sits at the tip of Seneca Lake, one of the "Finger Lakes," so named for their long, narrow shapes. The Glen is some 280 miles west of New York, a little less than a two hours' drive south of Syracuse through gorgeous terrain. Much like NASCAR's other road course, Watkins Glen is in an area famed for its wine.

Adjacent to Schuyler County, the home of The Glen, is Chemung County. More than wine, it is famous for some notable citizens. Mark Twain wrote *Tom Sawyer* and *Huckleberry Finn* while residing there, and is now buried in the county. Fashion designer Tommy Hilfiger and Heisman Trophy winner Ernie Davis also are from there.

To the NASCAR world, the most famous natives of Chemung are the Brothers Bodine—Geoffrey, Brett and Todd—whose parents operated Chemung Speedrome. They seldom visited The Glen because of their own racing careers. Brett Bodine said, "I didn't realize what Watkins Glen meant to the sporting car world at that time. ... It wasn't until I got to compete there that I realized how lucky I was to have lived so close to such a famous racetrack."

Drivers who have open-wheel experience usually feel more at home on road courses, which present many unique challenges. The Glen's "Esses" and undulating terrain require plenty of practice and patience for drivers whose background is rooted in racing on ovals.

Gone, But Not Forgotten

Nashville

International Speedway

Inaugural race:
August 10, 1958

Final Winston Cup race:
July 14, 1984

If you are 7 or 8 years old and you are spending your weekend nights at the racetrack, what sticks with you through the years are the assault on your senses. The tastes. The smells.

"The pizza," says Sterling Marlin. "The pizza was so good. And the smell of the popcorn. Of course, that's when we had to be up in the grandstands."

Then, after the races, "me and two or three buddies, we'd sneak through a hole

in the fence (and into the pits). You'd smell those old racecars, and the tire rubber. Fond memories," Marlin says softly.

Happily, Fairgrounds Speedway—once known as Nashville International Speedway—continues to make memories. It remains the site for late-model cars and modifieds and other modest racing ventures, though it now is overshadowed by the fancy new Nashville Superspeedway that opened in 2001 east of the city and quickly was awarded Busch Grand National, Craftsman Truck and Indy Racing events.

Neil Bonnett celebrated what he thought was a victory May 12, 1984, but Darrell Waltrip filed a protest and was awarded the win two days later. There was confusion because of a late wreck, and Bonnett passed Waltrip on the final lap though Waltrip was leading when the white and yellow flags flew.

Cup race here. "To tell you the truth, Winston Cup was probably there a year or two longer than it should have been, because we never did up the seating capacity," says Tom Roberts, once the track's public relations man.

But it was the other events, the weekly racing cards, that make this place so historic. Few, if any, short tracks produced so many Winston Cup drivers. The Nashville alumni association is astounding. This is where Darrell and Michael Waltrip got their start. Same

The Fairgrounds—"America's Favorite Short Track" is its slogan—is a .596-mile, neatly-banked asphalt oval at the Tennessee State Fair. It sits south of downtown Nashville on Nolensville Pike, not far from Greer Stadium, a baseball park with its trademark guitar-shaped scoreboard. They are a pair of anachronistic venues widely separated in distance and temperment from the ostentatious, modern, glass-and-steel downtown homes of the city's NFL and NHL franchises.

Greer Stadium is home to a Class AAA baseball team, the last stage of development for minor-leaguers headed to the majors. Fairgrounds Speedway has long served much the same purpose.

It was once a regular stop on the NASCAR circuit, from 1958 until July 14, 1984, when Geoffrey Bodine won the final Winston

with Sterling Marlin, his dad Coo Coo, Mike Alexander, Bobby Hamilton, Jeff Green and Casey Atwood.

Sterling, whose first race was at the Fairgrounds, and Alexander famously tangled here. One night, Marlin literally ran Alexander off the track. Alexander was injured in the incident but came back soon, and promoter Gary Baker set up a winner-take-all, 10-lap grudge match. Baker even dressed as a wrestling referee as he waved the green flag. Naturally, Marlin and Alexander tangled, and some of Alexander's sheet metal on the side began flapping in the wind. "Sterling done blow'd his doors off," said some of the locals. Sterling won the race, colleced $1,000—and a trophy shaped as the south end of a north-bound horse.

"It was *the* classic bullring," says Roberts, "a rock-'em, sock-'em short track."

It was and is a forgiving racetrack. With its wide, sweeping banks, looking uncannily like the brim of a Nashville singer's cowboy hat, it enables young drivers to learn side-by-side racing that flat tracks tend to inhibit. A quarter-mile oval track is encompassed inside the big speedway. Much of the infield area is truly a pit; it slopes to a sunken area, assuring spectators' line of sight isn't blocked by trucks and equipment. A massive scoreboard sits outside the exit of Turn 3. Billboards advertising less-than-premium beer and car parts and attorneys and radio stadiums ring the back stretch.

Fairgrounds Speedway still is a lovely place, its tidy grandstands of aluminum bleachers guarded by a metal roof overhang, grown a little rusty, and supported by a latticework of beams and girders. As fans walk from their cars up the hill to the stands, they pass one of those historical monuments more common to battlegrounds and roadways. It proclaims the speedway grounds as the site of harness racing as long ago as 1891.

The speedway is connected to the Exhibitor's Building of the State Fair; beyond lie other buildings and arenas typical of a fair. Alas, the famous wooden rollercoaster than rumbled just outside Turn 4 has been torn down since NASCAR's heyday here. The track itself is sheltered by grass berms on the Turn 4 side and backstretch. The typical chain-link fencing surrounds the track; in some spots, white vertical planks of wood have been inserted to the fence as blinds of sorts, to assure that all spectators are paying spectators.

Along the fence are regularly spaced signs of warning—"No trespassing or going under the fence: $250 fine."

You wonder if Sterling Marlin and his young pals were the reason those signs were placed there years ago.

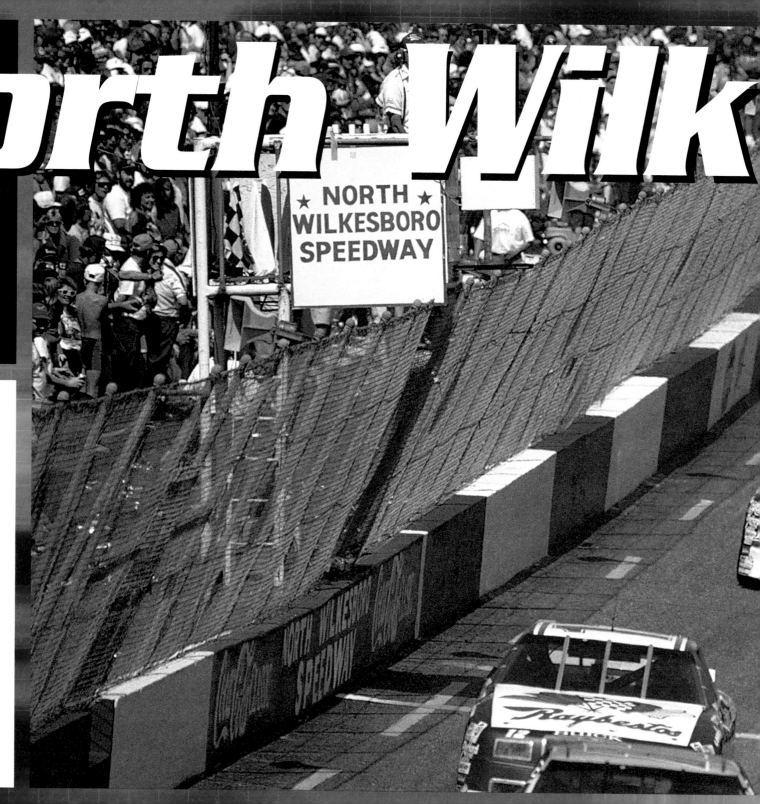

North Wilk
Speedway

Inaugural race:
October 16, 1949
Final Winston Cup race:
September, 29, 1996

D o not adjust your set. If you are watching some classic-sports race from North Wilkesboro Speedway, and it appears cars are running uphill, do not be alarmed. Your TV is fine.

They ARE running uphill.

Among the charms of North Wilkesboro, the backstretch incline—and the inevitable downhill ride on the front—was one of the most unique.

The slighty uphill grade emptied into the 14-degree

esboro

banking at the top of the .625-mile oval. The banking was high enough to make passing possible but not so much to keep it from being a precarious move. The Winston Cup garage area sat at the lower end of the infield, as if spilled into the corner by gravity. The cars spilled there, too, testing tires and physics and sheet metal and guts as they fought for the inside line, diving like fighter pilots as low and hard into Turn 1 as possible to maintain the inside line.

A media center barely larger than your dining room was only a few steps from the garage area. And there was a neat twist: victory lane sat atop the media center. The winning car wheeled onto an elevator outside the media center and was lifted to the roof level. The idea later was taken to Bristol, which employs the same fan-friendly view of the winner.

In this 1975 race, grandstands on the front stretch provided most of the seating. More seats were added later, but capacity reached only 40,000.

Modest grandstands streamed down the front stretch, and the owners tried to keep up with demands for tickets by adding more seats—even a section of bleachers the year it closed—but North Wilkesboro still seated only 40,000, and there wasn't room, money or interest in expanding the place with luxury boxes and more modern conveniences. It was a rough-hewn place, clearly out of step with the new tracks of the 1990s.

Let North Wilkesboro, one of the circuit's original tracks, stand as the most dramatic symbol of NASCAR growth, or greed, depending on your perspective.

The families of original owners Jack Combs and Enoch Staley were ready to sell the track in 1995. The Combs family sold its half to Bruton Smith for $6 million. The Staley clan sold to Bob Bahre for $8 million. However, Smith and Bahre were not able to agree on what to do with North Wilkesboro. So they let it rot rather than go into a partnership. "I think someday someone will have a race there," Bahre once told a reporter. "But it's probably going to be after Bruton and I are in heaven or hell."

Smith took one of the North Wilkesboro dates for his Texas Motor Speedway (capacity: 154,000-plus), and Bahre took a second date for New Hampshire (capacity: 91,000-plus). North Wilkesboro, small and remote— the most popular "secret" short-cut to the track shared by teams included a five-mile stretch on a dirt road—and ill-equipped for the sport's new millennium, was another victim of NASCAR's success.

The speedway was built in 1947, tucked in the foothills of the Smoky Mountains in western North Carolina, 70 or so miles northwest of Charlotte, near Highway 421 that leads from Winston-Salem up to ski resorts and tourist towns such as Boone and Blowing Rock. This was the site of the final race of the inaugural NASCAR season, called the "Strictly Stock Series." Bob Flock won the race, and Red Byron clinched the first series championship.

Wilkes County was home to the 19th-century villain Tom Dooley, the womanizing murderer who was memorialized in a Kingston Trio folk song in the 1960s. Wilkesboro boasts lovely, historic, Victorian-style homes dating as far back as the Civil War. The county has suffered financially as a result of the track's closing because some $50 million a year was pumped into the economy annually by the two races.

The area also was home to some villains of more innocuous crimes as the 1920s rolled around. This was moonshine country. The narrow, winding roads were the perfect proving ground for hot-footed 'shiners trying to outrun the "revenooers." The most famous was an easy-going, slow-talking youngster named Robert Glenn Johnson, Jr., who still lives near the speedway. Eighteen of Junior Johnson's 50 NASCAR wins came at this speedway. Some of the stories certainly are apocryphal, but there are legends about how friends of Junior's sitting in the stands conveniently provided debris on the track, forcing caution periods that enabled their man to catch up.

Johnson was immortalized in "The Last American Hero," a 1965 *Esquire* magazine piece by Tom Wolfe and the seminal bit of racing prose.

"Ten o'clock Sunday morning in the hills of North Carolina," Wolfe's piece began. "Cars, miles of cars, in every direction,

One of North Wilkesboro's trademarks established in the late 1970s was the Holly Farms sign that kept track of the race leaders.

millions of cars ... are all going to the stock car races, and that old mothering North Carolina sun keeps exploding off the windshields."

But the sun over North Wilkesboro set for good in 1996.

The last Winston Cup race here was September 29, 1996. Jeff Gordon was seeking a sweep of sorts. He had won on NASCAR's three other short tracks—Bristol, Martinsville and Richmond—but never at North Wilkesboro. He had been runner-up in the previous race there, to teammate Terry Labonte, who celebrated his record-tying 513th consecutive start that day.

Gordon held off Dale Earnhardt in the final event at North Wilkesboro, a relatively easy win.

"You don't want to see a place like this go, but at the same time, it's exciting to see how much this sport is growing. Who knows what level we'll reach," Gordon told reporters after the win.

Gordon acknowledged he wasn't terribly aware of North Wilkesboro's history, but some of the sport's veterans, such as Earnhardt, Darrell Waltrip and Benny Parsons, provided some lessons and lore that week.

"Learning all that from them sure makes me appreciate winning the last race a lot more," Gordon said. "Anyone who never won here in Winston Cup probably isn't going to get the chance now."

Riverside
International Raceway

Inaugural race:
Crown America 500, June 1, 1958

Final Winston Cup race:
Budweiser 400, June 10, 1988

Up in the north corner, where the famous "esses" once wriggled across the dusty plain and up to the mountain, there is now Moreno Valley Mall at TownGate. There are banks and grocery stores and chain restaurants nearby. There is a greenspace in the heart of it all, with a playground and park benches. It is the typical, suburban-sprawl, money-devouring, generic shopping area found in any city anywhere in the country.

Except for a small cluster of streets in an older, middle-class neighborhood a few blocks away, with streets like Gurney Place and Yarborough Drive and Andretti Street and Penske Street, there are few tangible reminders of the history buried beneath the parking lots and stores and other shrines of American consumer excess.

Even the relic, the enormous sign that withstood the track demolition and stubbornly stood for years to mark the area as the one-time site of Riverside International Raceway, is gone. In the ultimate irony, it fell victim when construction began in 2002 on a Lowe's Home Improvement Warehouse, a company intimately involved with NASCAR.

It's pretty much flat ground now. The mountain onto which the track reached was sheared. There are only a few slight rises and dips as shoppers navigate the area on a "ring road" around the mall. "It goes all the way around the mall. It's sort of like a race track," says a mall employee, trying to provide some consolation.

Riverside hosted racing for 30 years, from its first race in 1958 to its final race in 1988.

There was nothing quite like the racetrack that was Riverside International, with three decades of thrills and momentous moments. It was, according to Don Fuller's eulogy for the place in *AutoWeek* magazine after its final race in 1988, a "tough, mean, dirty, hot, dusty, windy, nasty miserable ol' place in the California desert."

From the start-finish line near the lower left-hand corner of the course, it made a slight bend to the left, then introduced the "esses," the series of subtle S-shaped turns that were the track's

signature. They ran up the mountain and to Turn 6, a hairpin right followed by a similar downhill hairpin left turn that is now mimicked in the "Carousel" at Infineon Raceway.

Turn 8 was a slightly broader right that spilled into a 1.1-mile straightaway. Speeds of 200-mph plus were not uncommon on the straightaway. Then ... careful. Better get on the brakes in a hurry and grab the gearshift for that slight hitch at the end that led to the tight, banked Turn 9 that swung around back to the start-finish line and pit road.

Riverside was built on the site of an old turkey farm, right off Highway 60, halfway between Los Angeles and Palm Springs. It was close enough to be accessible to L.A., some 70 miles northwest, but far enough away to seemingly avoid the clutches of its ever-expanding growth.

Riverside hosted its first race in September, 1957, then welcomed NASCAR the following year. Eddie Gray won the Crown America 500 race, but it was a bigger name—Parnelli Jones—who qualified No. 1. Because of geography and because the road course was more amenable to all forms of racing, Riverside hosted the most famous drivers from all venues, like Jones, from NASCAR, IndyCar, Grand Prix and sports cars.

It was a natural place, then, for a brainchild of some of racing's most forward-thinkers, including Les Richter, the former L.A. Rams lineman who was Riverside's president and general manager for 20 years. They created the International Race of Champions, which put drivers from different types of racing in identical cars. The first three IROC events were held there October 27-28, 1973. Unlike

Riverside was called by one writer a "tough, mean, dirty, hot, dusty, windy, nasty miserable ol' place in the California desert."

the NASCAR-dominated fields of IROC's evolution into the 1990s, this was pure variety pack. In order of their finish in the inaugural race: Mark Donohue, Bobby Unser, Peter Revson, George Follmer, Denis Hulme, A.J. Foyt, Richard Petty, Roger McCluskey, David Pearson, Gordon Johncock, Bobby Allison and Emerson Fittipaldi.

Allison was the most successful NASCAR driver at Riverside, with six wins. Richard Petty, Dan Gurney and Darrell Waltrip won five apiece. Some significant careers also got a boost there. Tim Richmond won his first two NASCAR Winston Cup races there, in 1982, and Ricky Rudd and Bill Elliott captured their maiden wins the following season.

Riverside also robbed NASCAR of one of its greats. "Little Joe" Weatherly was an irrepressible driver of the 1950s and 1960s, a practical joker who once filled rival Curtis Turner's in-car water jug with mint juleps before a race. Weatherly survived a German

sniper's bullet during World War II that knocked out two of his teeth, but he couldn't survive a 1964 accident at Riverside.

In those days, the area around the speedway was called Sunnymead. The largest city nearby was Riverside. But Los Angeles kept expanding. Riverside International Raceway wasn't nearly so remote any more. The desert wasn't nearly so formidable a foe for development. More people began to move there.

In 1984, Moreno Valley became officially incorporated. Six years later, it was designated the fastest-growing city in the United States. By then, Riverside International Raceway had become a casualty to the growth.

When the city was incorporated, a slogan was adopted:

"People, pride, progress."

Sometimes, the latter comes at a cost. In this instance, it came as a cost to a city's history, and the history of an entire sport.